An Unrequited Love

AN UNREQUITED LOVE:

AN EPISODE IN THE LIFE OF BEETHOVEN.

(FROM THE DIARY OF A YOUNG LADY.)

BY

LUDWIG NOHL.

TRANSLATED BY

ANNIE WOOD.

LONDON:
RICHARD BENTLEY & SON, NEW BURLINGTON STREET,
Publishers in Ordinary to Her Majesty the Queen.
1876.

LONDON:
PRINTED BY WILLIAM CLOWES AND SONS,
STAMFORD STREET AND CHARING CROSS.

𝔇𝔢𝔡𝔦𝔠𝔞𝔱𝔢𝔡

TO

HER MOST GRACIOUS MAJESTY

QUEEN VICTORIA,

WITH THE PROFOUND RESPECT OF THE

AUTHOR.

AN UNREQUITED LOVE.

AN EPISODE IN THE LIFE OF BEETHOVEN.

CHAPTER I.

In the year 1857 the Leipzig weekly paper *Die Grenzboten* published, under the title, "From the Years of Beethoven's Life," extracts from the diary of a young lady, which attracted at the time universal attention by their unpretending style. They were put together in the most simple way by the writer herself, and filled up from memory: the original was kept in reserve. Now, however, the lady is dead, and the diary has been handed to me with the permission to publish from it whatever is calculated to throw light on Beethoven's life and character.

But it is not only the reflection of Beethoven's

character in the clear mirror of this gentle but keenly sensitive soul, but also what was not to be seen there, the womanly soul itself, which, notwithstanding the timid modesty of her nature and the fragmentary form of these notes, awakens our deepest sympathy. Beethoven's genius, the nobility of his sentiments, the natural kindliness and simple force of character which distinguished him, in a word, his intense humanity, come out clearly before us in these extracts, and make us understand how in close personal intercourse, such a nature must have made a deep and almost overpowering impression on this lady.

But it is interesting to observe how, after a time, the tender preference of her heart became purified from all selfish considerations, and was transformed into a deep and sincere feeling of friendship, full of veneration, and eager anxiety to be useful. We have also a very evident proof that the musician, absorbed in his genius, had but a slight appreciation of the unobtrusive and faithful assistance in real life offered to him in the family and in the person of this young lady. In truth, he was not very grateful for it. Indeed, he considered his private opinion and his own wish to be as infallible in matters which lay beyond his province as was his insight into the conditions and laws of his own artistic creations. Thus, we see, as it were, with our own eyes, the threads of the sad destiny spun and drawn round his head, prepared for him by the adoption of his notorious nephew, which eventually brought about the catastrophe in that mournful drama of life. The shadow which thenceforward darkened the later years of the great master is distinctly discernible in these records kept by a third person, and forms the tragical background, against which this otherwise calm idyllic scene in private life is played out.

The following remarks will suffice to introduce the subject.

Señor Giannatasio del Rio, a Spaniard by birth, together with his wife, a native of Italy, formerly a tutor in a noble house, had, since the year 1798, conducted a boys' school in

Vienna. In 1815, by the will of his younger brother Karl, Beethoven was appointed guardian of the only surviving son, who was called Karl, after his father. The child was then eight years old. His mother, on account of her irregular life, was excluded from all power over his education, and Beethoven being a bachelor, and not possessing a household of his own, the court decided that the little lad should be sent to school, and his uncle fixed upon Giannatasio's establishment, which had been specially recommended to him.

The domestic management of this house was in the hands of a conscientious but invalid mother and her two daughters. Fanny, the elder, born 26th of May 1790, was consequently at that time twenty-five years of age, and the writer of our diary; and Nanni, two years younger, was betrothed to Herr Leopold von Schmerling, the father of the present possessor of these extracts. The latter thus describes "auntie" and her sister :—

"In her youth she must have been very

pretty, though not so much so as my mother, her sister Nanni, who was an acknowledged beauty. From all that I have heard, Beethoven appears to have admired my mother, but she was then betrothed to my father.

"Auntie was short, my mother of ordinary height, auntie's hair was brown, my mother's much darker, almost black. Auntie had greenish blue eyes, with a lovely expression in them, sometimes dreamy, sometimes animated. My mother's eyes were a very bright brown, full of fire, or softness, according to her emotion. It was often affirmed that southern blood flowed in my mother's veins, because she was so very vivacious and capable of such intense and deep feeling. My aunt's was a calmer and very shy nature. She often told me that, when a young girl, from sheer embarrassment, she would talk on continuously, and then become so confused that she finally ran away.

"My aunt's character was essentially melancholy; on the other hand, my mother's was peculiarly cheerful. At times, auntie could be merry too, and she was specially addicted to writing comic poems. Whenever anything very ludicrous occurred in the family, she would turn it into doggerel rhyme."

The melancholy appears, however, to have been the result of internal organisation, and to have depended chiefly on physical causes, for we read that "my poor aunt's mind was affected seven times in her life, when she fell into a state of deep melancholy. Each time she recovered she seemed to be in heaven, as if a cloud had fallen from her spirit." One of these attacks is mentioned as early as 1812 in the diary. The malady lasted eight months, then suddenly her mind became quite clear again. One characteristic feature of her mind was a very remarkable, yet inexpressibly intense delight in natural beauty, as if she had instinctively sought and found in its harmony the healing virtues her nature required. Beethoven also possessed this peculiarity, as exemplified in the Pastoral Symphony.

The year previous to that in which our

extracts begin, Fanny's mind had sustained a great shock from the death of her betrothed. She remained unmarried all her life, which was prolonged to the age of eighty-three.

Her character is best described by Goethe's beautiful lines on Gretchen :—

> "Und all ihr häusliches Beginnen
> Umfangen in der kleinen Welt."

If, however, our great "homeless one," rushing from one artistic achievement to another, a true Faust, dashed to atoms the rocks of the hitherto accepted canons of art; if he smiled at the young housekeeper going about with her key-basket, and said jestingly, "Here comes the Lady Abbess!" she confesses that it did not please her much.

On the other hand, solid German culture was everywhere apparent in this house, besides an earnest pursuit of all that was beautiful and ennobling in intellectual and artistic life. The best evidence of the deep culture and inward vitality which distinguishes the German, and especially the Austrian, is the spirited cultivation of the art which is the surest test of inward life and its development—music.

On this point the possessor of the diary writes of the two sisters as follows :—" Both had fine soprano voices, but my aunt's was the deeper of the two. Fräulein Frölich, who was once betrothed to Grillparzer, whom I met lately, still speaks with enthusiasm of a recitative and aria from 'Titus,' which my aunt used to sing so wonderfully. I myself heard aunt sing the aria from 'Freischütz' with the Prighiera, when she was sixty years of age, and she sang it with the greatest spirit and most finished execution. She was certainly endowed with wonderful musical talents. In her youth she sang duets with Schubert. Small operas used to be performed in my grandfather's house, in which my mother and aunt sang the principal parts."

But one thing of great importance we learn from the diary itself, that Mozart's and Beethoven's divine compositions were sung by preference, a fact of no mean significance sixty years ago.

As a decided proof that such music was really appreciated, and had been cultivated to a high degree in the family, we have the following simple record. On the 29th November 1814, at a concert in honour of the guests of the Vienna Congress, Beethoven's music only was performed.

"*December 3rd.*—On Tuesday, Beethoven's masterpieces enchanted every one. This spark of divine fire inspires me with admiration."

Besides the 'Battle of Vittoria' and the 'Glorious Moment,' the Seventh Symphony was played on this occasion, though at that time it was far beyond the comprehension of "connoisseurs." If we were to inquire into the motive which induced this young lady to begin a diary—as it is not an ordinary matter to keep a record of one's experiences in life— we are answered on the very first page.

"*January 1st*, 1812.—It has long been my earnest wish to keep a diary, but time and circumstances have hitherto hindered the fulfilment of my desire. Even this book will scarcely be a diary. I shall merely note down many a happy hour, also many a sorrowful one. Such recollections always bring me pleasure. The former look all the brighter in retrospect, and the remembrance of even unpleasant hours is often pleasant!"

No doubt these reminiscences would have been limited to the narrow groove of her individual existence, but for the sudden introduction of a personage who invests them with a world-wide interest, and justifies our interest in the most secret mysteries of private feeling and emotion. A living breath of the mighty inspiration which animates Beethoven's art, and which has renewed the creative power of art throughout the age, will be found in these extracts, pure and maidenly as they are, and confined within the sphere of womanly perception. But that which enables the writer to comprehend something of the genius of the great master, or rather of his deeper spiritual life and nature, and in some measure to express them in words, was the habit she had acquired of studying her own inner life, thus enabling her to obtain a clue to the secret of all human existence. We shall understand this better by following the extracts themselves.

We owe to her the details of the circumstances which brought down this genius from the "glorious but lonely height" of his artist-existence into the refreshing intimacy of real family life.

During the time of the Congress, Hofrath Duncker, Secretary of State to Frederick William III. of Prussia, resided in the house of Giannatasio, and was on terms of friendly intercourse with the young ladies. He accompanied their music, and read poetry aloud to them, amongst which was a tragedy, 'Leonore Prohaska.' He was also a great admirer and worshipper of Beethoven, and the girls obtained from him many particulars about the master whom they already reverenced so highly, and who had just been raised to the highest pinnacle of earthly glory, by the performance of his music before the Congress, and by the reception of his

'Fidelio' in his second and adopted home, *Vienna*. "To-day our dear Duncker made us very happy by presenting 'Fidelio' to us. How doubly precious is this gift to me!" writes Fanny on the 25th of January 1815. Duncker had begged Beethoven to set his tragedy to music, and had frequent interviews with him on the subject. The four bars which the great master composed for this purpose are still in the possession of the descendants of Giannatasio. The design was never carried out, and the fragment remained in manuscript. The young ladies were very anxious to become acquainted with Beethoven, for Duncker had told them a great deal of his nobility and goodness, and the beginning of the acquaintance is thus described:—

"*January* 25*th*, 1816.—What I have often vainly wished for, that Beethoven should come to our house, has at length happened. Yesterday afternoon he brought his little nephew to see the Institute; and to-day everything is arranged. Of my childish embarrassment I will say nothing. Many thoughts were running in my head, and the auspices were so unfavourable that I may be excused if I was absent.

"I cannot describe the delight I feel at being thus brought into communion with a man whom I honour so much as an artist, and esteem so highly as a man. It seems like a dream that my wishes are at last realised. How delighted I should be if we could really enter into friendly relations with Beethoven, and if I might hope to make a few hours of his life pleasant to him —to him who has banished so many dark clouds from mine. The intense sympathy I feel for him in his sad condition of deafness is the principal reason for wishing it.

"The young man who was with him (the poet and author, Karl Bernard) said to Nanni, 'Beethoven will often visit you.' One would almost think he had divined how much we wish for it. In this hope life has become an enjoyment to me, and I now feel a deep interest in the prospect of the days to come."

We gather from these few lines that a stronger

feeling was at work here than the mere curious interest in the "great man" which many so-called educated persons cherish for artists. It is rather an enthusiastic sympathy with his intellectual and artistic nature, which, while it had inspired the wish for his personal acquaintance, decided the impression made by it, and stamped, as it were, the moment of the first meeting as an important crisis in the family circle, but more particularly to Fanny herself. But in order thoroughly to understand this impression, and duly to appreciate the value of the communications we are about to make, it is well to have a clear idea of the great master who stands before us, of the importance of his artistic creations, and of his intellectual efforts. To this end, a glance over his gradual development up to this point will be our surest guide. The following chapter contains a sketch of his career, according to the most recent researches, to the time of his meeting personally with our heroine.

CHAPTER II.

AN ARTIST'S CAREER.

Laufet, Brüder, eine Bahn
Freudig, wie ein Held, zum Siegen.
Schiller.

LUDWIG VAN BEETHOVEN was born at Bonn, on the Lower Rhine, in the year 1770.

That was the epoch in Europe, and especially in Germany, when the human mind, even in the outer circles of the people, was awakening to a consciousness of itself, and beginning to inquire not only after the supply of its needs, but for a fixed aim for its whole existence. Science, and especially philosophy, went hand in hand with practical attempts to give a better direction to our outward life. Originating in England, and fomented by the American Declaration of Independence and the French

Revolution, that great movement of minds arose to which we are indebted for all that we now possess, and towards which we are still striving in the better conduct of our lives.

This spirit, emanating from the heart as from the east, from France in her demand for freedom as from Prussia determinately forcing herself into eminence, spread to the Lower Rhine, and even in the small electoral capital city, Bonn, gave a fresh impulse to life. Maximilian Franz, youngest son of Maria Theresa, and brother of Frederick the Great's admirer, Joseph II., embodied the spirit of the time there by founding a new university, and encouraging the development of art and theatrical representation. In addition to Beethoven, a special favourite with this gifted prince, these advantageous circumstances called forth a goodly number of distinguished men, who, at a later period, spread not only over the whole of Germany, but beyond it. Beethoven himself, unquestionably the greatest of them all, was impelled to raise his art—which he selected from natural inclination, and because it was his father's and grandfather's vocation, both superior men—to a place among the nobler efforts of the human intellect, and to exalt music to the loftiest height of which it has yet been capable, by making it the real expression of our inner life. How this goal was striven for by the very young musician, who even then wrote, "If I ever become a great man," &c., and how it was attained by the mature man, is the essence of his artistic creations, as also of his life. It is to his truly untiring energy in the pursuit of this aim that we of the present generation owe, not only Beethoven's works themselves, but the mighty impulse which he, above all, gave to the highest efforts of the German nation in the direction of musical art. For himself, he owed to it the truly tragical yet heroic fate of which later on we shall have to consider some significant turns and windings.

It was, in the first instance, the impulse to emulate vigorously his great predecessors in the art, and the earnest desire to make himself master of the methods which they had pursued, which drew him away from the Rhine, with its intellectual activity, to the Danube, which had taken a less stirring part in that phase of our development. But at Bonn, in addition to the Shakespearian representations and the poetry of Lessing, Goethe, and Schiller, in which the North German intellectual life is expressed and completed, music was supported, especially since Max Franz, by the truly great tragical composer, Gluck, and the most human of all artists, Mozart. Hence a musician so profoundly earnest as Beethoven was, even in his early years, could not but feel that springs were flowing here which were sufficient to supply one side of life, nay, even life itself, in all its depths. Therefore, away to Vienna, where the "water of life" was to be drawn for his individual genius. A first visit to the imperial city in 1787 led to a personal acquaintance with Mozart, who had given him a few lessons, and bestowed on him his blessing as a musician. It was of him that he prophesied, "Mark that young man; he will make to himself a name in the world." But, on the whole, the sojourn in Vienna, and even the meeting with Mozart, who was then absorbed in the composition of 'Don Juan,' was not productive of any immediate result, beyond the irresistible longing to return thither soon, and to remain there permanently. Unfavourable circumstances delayed this till the year 1792. His mother's illness, which recalled him suddenly from Vienna, ended, after bitter domestic suffering, with her death. His father, a tenor of the electoral court, had inherited from his own mother a propensity for drink, and was banished to a small provincial town. Ludwig received the half of his little income, out of which he had to feed, clothe, and educate his younger brothers, Karl and Johann. What the artist lost from want of regular culture, the man gained in his inner development. The duties of a man lay on the shoulders of a boy scarcely sixteen. But he fulfilled them, and not until he had fulfilled them did he devote himself completely again to his studies as an artist. Haydn's passage through

Bonn impelled him to carry out the visit to Vienna; and the "old papa" was to be teacher of the court organist, Mozart being now dead. Thus the musician, at the age of twenty-one, visited Vienna for the second time, never again to leave it. He became the pupil of Haydn, of Schenk, the composer of the merry 'Village Barber,' of Salieri, and of the learned but dry master of counterpoint, Albrechtsberger. The thoroughness with which he fulfilled the duties of actual life he now brought to bear on his art, and no exertions were spared till he was absolutely at home in its language, and had completely mastered it.

For what had he not to express? This was what musical Vienna, the mother of all true poetry in this direction, at once felt, and she loudly applauded him as the successor of Gluck, Haydn, and Mozart, especially when he played his own compositions. He floated at once, at least as a musical performer, on the spring tide of public favour, and thereby of material prosperity. His free, bold, high-soaring spirit enchanted the really cultivated people of Vienna, it being something of the true spirit of the time which prevailed there. "Freedom, youth, independence," seemed the cry of the 'Sonate Pathétique' which soon belonged to the whole world. It expressed in full, powerful tones what he himself had lived, felt, and experienced on the free Rhine, and what had long slumbered in his breast, till he had acquired the complete leisure and outward security necessary for the pure expression of his inner self.

And thus ripe earnestness and real activity developed in him, according to the greeting which Schiller offers to the age of art and to artists themselves, to whose hands the dignity of mankind is intrusted—

> "Wie schön, o Mensch, mit deinem Palmenzweige
> Stehst du an des Jahrhunderts Neige
> In edler stolzer Männlichkeit,
> Mit aufgeschloss'nem Sinn, mit Geistesfülle,
> Voll milden Ernsts, in thatenreicher Stille,
> Der reifste Sohn der Zeit!
> Frei durch Vernunft, stark durch Gesetze,
> Durch Sanftmuth gross und reich durch Schätze,
> Die lange Zeit dein Busen dir verschwieg!"

This is the lofty ideal of human nature, the wide field of action, which, to the representative man, divests life of its accidental and transitory character, and rounds it to a worthy and harmonious whole. Such was the cherished aim of this artist. His art became to him the high and holy vocation of civilising men, and of revealing to them their inner selves. "Man must be ceaselessly active" was his axiom; and, as from a long pent-up fountain, countless streams of noble creations flowed henceforth from the hidden depths of his soul.

At the same time, considerable play was given to those lighter expressions of his art which add so much charm and delightful enjoyment to the more serious action of life. Songs and sonatas, as well as trios, quartettes, and symphonies—a perfect cornucopia of fresh musical delight—were poured out upon the world, lost in admiring astonishment.

Meanwhile his own concentrated purpose was bent upon the deed of a noble, proud manliness, on which the improvement of the age and the salvation of the world seemed to depend. The eyes of all thoughtful men were fixed upon the great star of freedom which rose in the French Revolution.

And when its object and ideas took form in the person of one single man—at once Man and Deed—when the young general Buonaparte by his brilliant victories carried idolised "Liberty" into every land, then it was that all hearts burst forth into flame for this hero of liberty, who was to bring back the most glorious times of history. Certainly no consul of the great Roman Republic appeared greater than this figure of the first general, so soon to be First Consul, of the new French Republic.

Then what more natural than that Beethoven's heart should glow with sympathy when, in the year 1798, General Bernadotte, the future king of Sweden, then French ambassador in Vienna, in his unbounded admiration for Napoleon, proposed to the great musician, who met him, and whose heroic nature he must have recognised, to erect a monument in his own art to the greatest man of the time?

And he did so—in such manner as far to outshine all other memorials of the great French ruler in greatness and in permanence, for it was dedicated to the intellect which all competent judges allow to this wonderful man. The Third Symphony ('Eroica'), which, arose out of this proposal, was not completed till five years later, yet it represents to us the spirit which animated Beethoven's early manhood. This, greater and truer than the spirit of Napoleon himself, overcame its later aberrations, and never ceased to inspire the artist to glorious creations.

But soon, greater, deeper things presented themselves.

"Free through reason!" This youthful, bold Siegfried accepted this exclamation in its literal meaning, and, conscious of his own powers; and carried away by the stream of lofty endeavours, he disregarded the limits which an inevitable necessity sets to our reason, our will. "Thou shalt trample upon the serpent's head, and he shall bruise thy heel!" says the most ancient oracle.

Utter recklessness of his physical condition, especially in moments of highest inspiration, early undermined his bodily health, and, what was worse, affected the sense which, as he himself says, "I need in a much higher degree than others, which I once possessed in perfection, in a perfection such as few of my profession have or ever have had!" And, when the first symptoms of such neglect of health began to show themselves, he cried out, "Courage! Notwithstanding all bodily infirmities, my intellect must reign twenty-five years—there they are; this year must surely decide that I am of full age."

But we learn more of his inner feelings concerning the terrible form of sorrow which darkened his life, through the sustained knocking motive of the first movement of the C flat Symphony. "So fate knocks at my door!" he observed, more than twenty years later, of this motive, which is characterised by such manly confidence and daring resolution. This movement dates from the same time as the First Quartettes (op. 18), and now and again reveals the gloomy and often wildly sorrowful spirit of the musician, so early and so heavily visited by fate, out of which a powerful and ideal faith in our happiness and a high and noble view of the world and humanity were to be developed.

Even at this period he seemed to foresee such a solution of his sorrow, for it was then that the Adagio of that Fifth Symphony was written, with all its irresistible rush of conscious, intense happiness.

He had found a high track; it might lead to the highest things. His contemporaries discovered in his early sonatas and concertos "many beauties;" in the favourite septette, "a great deal of taste and feeling;" in his First Symphony, "much art, novelty, and wealth of ideas." The eyes of the friends of art, as well as those of the admiring crowd, were fixed upon him; they expected great things, even after Haydn and Mozart. But no one knew what was then occupying the mind of the great musician, and leading him to the most terrible despair, to the very brink of the grave.

He wrote on the 1st of June 1801 to a confidential friend in Courland, whom he urged to come to Vienna, "For your Beethoven is very unhappy, at strife with nature and Creator." Then followed the fearful declaration, which only the deepest misery and bitterest disturbance of his whole being could bring forth, "Too often have I cursed Him for exposing His creatures to be the sport of accident, so that often the noblest blossom is blighted and crushed by it." But a few weeks later, he addressed another confidential friend, a physician, Dr. Wegeler, at Bonn, and, after imploring help and counsel from him, adds, "I may truly say, my life is a misery to me. For almost two years I have avoided all society, because it is not possible for me to tell people I am deaf! I have again and again cursed my existence. Plutarch has taught me resignation. I will, if possible, bid defiance to my fate, though there are moments of my life when I am the most wretched being on God's earth."

When his friend wrote sympathisingly, and

begged for further news, he replied, on the 16th of November 1801, that on the whole he was better, but "this calamity!" "Oh, I would compass the world, were I free from this!" he exclaimed. "My youth, I feel, is beginning now. Every day I approach nearer the goal which I feel, but cannot describe. Only in thus striving can your Beethoven live. Speak not of rest! You shall yet see me as happy as it is permitted to us here below to be—that is, not unhappy! No, I could not endure it. I will seize Fate by the throat, it shall not quite bow me down. Oh, how beautiful it is to live life a thousand times!" We have yet to learn what a new and sweet happiness was to be added, by the love of a "dear enchanting girl:" for to whom was love more necessary than to him who "must drag on his life drearily and sadly," since the envious demon, bad health, had played him false? This happiness beams and sparkles in his musical productions. What is all that he had hitherto expressed of man's inner life compared to the Sonata in D flat, op. 31, ii., the wonderfully dramatic agitated first movement of which distinctly belonged to the autumn of 1801, and appears to talk in personal speech of personal things? Compared to such heart poetry, what is his 'Adelaida,' which, even at that time, was universally loved for its pure breathing tenderness? Yet, it was only a graceful clear echo of Mozart's flute-like tones of love and happiness. But, true and beautiful as are Mozart's melodies, the first expression of jubilant enjoyment of life springing out of love and happiness is in the D flat Sonata, rendered into original words by Beethoven, and out of what a depth of earnest striving, out of what a depth of sorrow on account of this high striving!

Yet she, whose love caused new life to spring out of suffering, was false to him. We shall hear of this again. He to whom love appeared the crowning happiness of life must have highly prized fidelity.

After a short respite, the difficulty of hearing returned, and with it the most frightful disturbance of mind. If there be one to whom

Bethoven's tones do not speak—and what human mind can be insensible to them?—at least the writing will appeal to him which he composed on the 6th of October 1802, at the village of Heiligenstadt, near Vienna, and which, being addressed to his two brothers as his heirs, has received the name of the Heiligenstadt testament.

"Oh you men, who look upon me as being unfriendly, sullen, or misanthropical, what injustice you do me; you who do not know the secret cause. My heart has been from childhood full of tenderness and benevolence. I was ever inclined to perform great actions. But only think that during the last six years an incurable misfortune has befallen me! Born with a social disposition, I was obliged early to isolate myself and to spend my life alone."

Then he goes on to tell how that summer some one was once standing beside him, his pupil, Ferdinand Ries, and heard a flute in the distance, but *he* heard nothing. "Such things drive me to despair; it would not take much to induce me to put an end to my life," he adds, "only my art restrains me, and it is impossible to leave the world before I have finished all I feel capable of doing."

Then he goes on to dispose of his little property—the most valuable of which was a quartette of stringed instruments, now in the Berlin Library—and thus addresses his brothers: "Teach your children to seek virtue, which can alone make them happy, and not riches! I speak from experience. It supported me in my misery, next of course, to my art; and to it I owe the not putting an end to my own life. Farewell—love one another."

He concludes with, "If death comes before I have been able to develop all my powers, it will come too soon. But, I am content. Will it not free me from a state of constant suffering? Come when thou wilt, I will meet thee bravely."

So deeply did this sorrow penetrate his life that, a few days later, he again seized the pen, hitherto devoted to the service of his music, and poured out a truly harrowing confession of the sorrow of his life.

"I take leave of thee with sadness. Yes! I feel compelled to give up the cherished hope of partial recovery which I brought with me here. Hope has faded from me, even as dead leaves fall in autumn dry and withered. The courage the lovely summer gave me is gone—gone!" He adds, "It is long since I felt the glow of real happiness. When, oh when, shall I feel it again in the temple of nature and of mankind? Never? That would be too hard!"

What did the world know of this man's suffering? In the following year, 1803, he appeared again, and announced that, in spite of all hindrances of nature, "he could still be a worthy artist and man, and that his courage had not failed him." He expressed this in the Second Symphony, which he had composed during that sad autumn at Heiligenstadt. And though the public rather wondered at the new work than understood it, yet they had a vague consciousness of something new, daring, and sublime in its spirit. One of the reporters, rising to the comprehension of the power displayed in his earlier works, and in commenting upon the oratorio 'Christ on the Mount of Olives,' remarked :—" It confirms my long-cherished opinion that Beethoven in course of time will contribute to the revolution in music as much as Mozart. He is hastening with great strides towards the goal."

But when a " great stride," even one of the greatest, came before the world—the Adagio of the Third Symphony ('Eroica')—the sorrow of the above confessions found expression, and rose to the grand interpretation of the limitation and transitoriness of all that is great and true in the world, people found in it too much of the startling and exceptional, and accused him of striving after originality rather than real beauty and grandeur. Beethoven is said to have answered, when the length of his symphony was complained of, that if he wrote one to last an hour, they ought to find it short enough! Beethoven did not care in the least

D

for public applause. He knew what suffering and struggle, what encouragement to noble efforts he had worked into this full expression of his genius, and what it was worth; hence what need had he to care for the capricious crowd?

But had *he* remained worthy of it, he to whom the work was dedicated, with the simplest inscription: " Buonaparte—Ludwig van Beethoven"? A record exists, too characteristic of Beethoven's estimate of art, as well as of human life, to be omitted here. His pupil, Ries, relates:—"I was the first to bring him the tidings that Buonaparte had been declared Emperor, whereupon he burst into a rage, and exclaimed, 'After all, then, he is only an ordinary man. Now he will trample all human rights under foot to serve his ambition. He will now place himself higher than all others, and become a tyrant!'" And going to the table, Beethoven seized the title-page at the top, tore it in two, and threw it on the ground. The first page was re-written, and a new title given to the Symphony, 'Sinfonia Eroica.' This was manly wrath!

But the enthusiasm for human right and freedom expressed here represented in noble harmony and rhythm the heroic life of such a mighty mover of the world. In the solemnity of his death it was not lost, and soon found an opportunity to form a suitable background for true and noble action.

Meanwhile, the intrinsic greatness announced in the earliest works of Beethoven had not remained hidden.

The performance of 'Christ on the Mount of Olives,' in the spring of 1803, brought the composer a commission to write a new opera for the Vienna stage, on conditions which promised him an existence free from pecuniary difficulties. But outward circumstances hindered the execution of this plan. But in the year 1804, when the 'Eroica' had come to the hearing of connoisseurs, the new director of the theatre offered him a similar commission. The result was 'Fidelio.'

Need we write a word upon the beauties of this immortal work? A noble defender of freedom languishes in prison through the violence of a personal enemy. His wife, Leonora, disguises herself as a man, becomes an attendant in the prison, and frees her husband at the moment when the "murderer" is about to accomplish his death, and frees with him all the other prisoners equally suffering under political tyranny. "The brother seeks his brothers!" and "kills his wife first!" indicate the whole atmosphere and the impulse to bold, manly action, even in weak woman. Where "humanity and kindness reign," there also springs the noblest love and most self-sacrificing fidelity towards the loved one.

Could any one fail to understand this lofty conception of the time, written as it was with the composer's very heart's blood? The French invasion of Vienna in 1805 interfered with the success of the work, and after remodelling it in 1806, the composer withdrew it from the stage, in the momentary fancy that it was not appreciated, or not satisfactorily performed. But the main impression of it remained fixed in the minds of all those who had music in their hearts as part of the life of humanity, especially that pure model of instrumental art, the overture to 'Leonora.'

But these "hearts" were not in a position to draw the composer into full light, and to give him his right place in art and life. So, after the apparent shipwreck of his best efforts, he withdrew into the solitude of his own world in deep melancholy. Yet he felt high capabilities within him; felt himself called to still higher and greater things than he had yet accomplished. Should he despair of a life which appointed to him such a lofty task, and laid upon him such noble activity?

Boldly his free spirit strove against the fate of outer limitation, as exemplified in the manly self-assertion, the summoning of his own power and might in the first movement of the C flat Symphony, which had never before been heard so distinctly in the language of music. Did he not triumph? Even through the wondrous sadness of the Adagio there is trustful resignation, inward certainty of victory. For where, hitherto, had been heard such trumpet sounds of jubilant power and enrapturing glory, celebrating the sure victory of our better will, as in the finale of this symphony?

In this symphony (Fifth) Beethoven is born, the great, free, courageous Beethoven, whose power is light from within, whose shield is the high aim of humanity, freedom, happiness, self-reliance! The limitation, the suffering, is overcome. The sense of life has been awakened, with the power to free life from narrowing transitory influences, and to rise to imperishable good.

This Beethoven we must keep steadily before us, in order to understand his life and his sufferings. His existence is to be a constant, brave, and yet frequently hopeless struggle, and with his heart wounded to death, he seeks to find inward joy in the temple of nature and of men!

In the Pastoral Symphony, superscribed "Reminiscences of Country Life," we have the awakening of cheerful sensations on arriving in the country; a scene by the rippling brook, amid the quiet and peace of nature, and the joyful songs of birds, a merry gathering of peasants with dance and play; then the rising of the storm, and, when that is past, the shepherds' song of joy and gratitude to the Great Power who rules nature and human life.

The "Lord, we thank Thee" speaks more clearly than the purely instrumental "Shepherds' Hymn," than if, according to his original intention, words and chorus had come in, gaining at the same time a special and clearly defined expression in the First Mass which he wrote in 1807. But though this mass abounds in characteristic traits of the great master's feeling, intellect, and fancy, still it only touches the outward garment, the historical significance of Christianity, not its eternal meaning and essence. Indeed, we shall not be far wrong in ascribing more real religion, that is, more direct apprehension of a living Power, to the Pastoral Symphony than to the Mass in C sharp.

Later in the history of his life we meet with an encounter with his time and the world surrounding him, on which he was as dependent as the most simple being, but which he was in the habit of entirely forgetting while absorbed in his creations. On the 22nd of December 1808, the first performance of the Fifth and Sixth Symphonies took place. It revealed to the world, or at least the world of Vienna—then the Areopagus of musical questions—the true human beauty and the grand manly earnestness of the artist who held his music for a revelation "higher than all wisdom and philosophy."

The next event which Beethoven chose as an image of life was the glorious rising of Austria, that is, of the German nation against their hereditary foe, Napoleon, to whom the great musician had once erected so glorious a memorial.

Austria solemnised in 1809 its "war of freedom," the consequences of which were not apparent till the years 1813 and 1814, but whose first appeal to the German spirit was the true cause of the movement which, in the spring of 1813, began in the north, and soon spread over all Germany. It led to the general rising of the nation, the driving back of the enemy, and re-kindled the feeling of community of German spirit and life, the fruits of which we are beginning to enjoy now.

And it was this which inspired Beethoven's genius anew, while the electric movement was thrilling through the people of Austria, rousing all to action, and each one to self-sacrifice. It was one of the most joyful moments of the whole Austrian life, for the nation itself stood to arms, not the soldier by profession only, but the nation represented by princes and nobles, as well as by burghers and peasants. Its leader, the Archduke Charles, was a typical hero of such a general rising of a people for their deliverance, in spite of the battles of Aspern and Wagram, which, though no defeats in themselves, led to defeats in a political sense.

The exciting game of war for the defence of the Fatherland, and for the protection of wives and children, with the spirited gathering of the martial youth, was to Beethoven a picture of joyous elevation, not only of individual existence, but of life as a whole, of freedom and happiness, hence the production of the Seventh Symphony. Never before were heroic power and physical activity, with their result, certain victory, so wonderfully expressed as in this masterpiece of instrumental art. It was felt and acknowledged to be such, and was, so to speak, the first joyful flourish of trumpets announcing the revival of German life, victory, and also the first awakening of the German nation to a sense of its high vocation. When, now, the universal rising against Europe's common enemy began, and Wellington at Vittoria gained a decisive victory over him, then the wars' alarm of the last twenty years concentrated itself into a masterly expression, in which our great musician called to his aid all the resources of his art. And with this last phase of Beethoven's individual development, up to the point where we meet him personally, we draw to the close our biographical interlude.

He wrote the 'Battle of Vittoria,' which we have already named. The performance of this work, in December 1813, for the benefit of the wounded at Hanau, penetrated into the understanding of the masses, who hitherto had not been able to comprehend Beethoven's compositions truly, as he embued his works with the spirit of the times. The Seventh Symphony was received with joy by people now at liberty. "Long honoured at home and abroad, as one of the greatest composers of music, on this occasion Beethoven celebrated his triumph," says a critical journal; and even the *Wiener Zeitung*, devoted merely to politics, took notice of this performance, and said that the unanimous applause of the thronged hall was enthusiastic to rapture.

This was followed by the repetition of

'Fidelio.' The reconstruction of it, which the composer had done with his whole heart and his highest ability and knowledge, took the hearts of the public by storm, and disarmed criticism. " Again I admire Beethoven's glorious music in 'Fidelio,' writes Fräulein Giannatasio on the 7th of June 1814; and the great musician wrote in his diary of that spring, " Grant more nobility to my loftiest thoughts, lead them to truths which will remain true for eternity!" The papers announced that it was a "marvellous success;" that there was "stormy applause." The house, too, was always filled now, and there was an eager call for a new composition in a cheerful strain.

We can now quite understand that such an artist, of whom Vienna and all Austria were proud, should be called upon to co-operate in celebrating the "sacred moment" when the sovereigns of Europe met in the imperial city, to conclude a lasting peace. We have already mentioned the concert in honour of the guests at the Congress of Vienna. Upwards of six thousand persons filled the hall, representing the *élite* of the city and of all Europe, and to their high social state the culture which might fairly be regarded as characteristic of the age corresponded.

"The respectful withdrawal of all noisy signs of applause gave it the character of a great religious solemnity. Every one seemed to feel that such an occasion would never return in his life," reports one who was present. But this eye-witness forgot to mention that the excitement repeatedly broke through the restraint of an etiquette which allowed no manifestation of applause in the presence of royal personages. Even the *Wiener Zeitung* acknowledged that there was a moment when the delight of all present burst forth in such thunders of applause as to overpower the strong accompaniment of the composer.

How Beethoven himself regarded this artistic action of his, and what was to him the final aim of it, is told us in his own journal with the simpleness of a great and true soul.

"Let all that is called life be sacrificed to noble aims, and to a sanctuary of art."

The next record is evidently dated at the time of that grand production which, while it placed the result of his own thoughts before the world, had at the same time lighted up his own way, and warned him to be true to the end, till the aim of his suffering and exhausting life should be attained at last.

"To set the ear machine travelling, and then, if possible, to travel! This I owe to myself, to men, and to the Almighty. Only thus can I develop all that is latent within me. A little court and a small band of musicians to perform the music written by me, and then to the honour of the Great, the Eternal, the Everlasting!"

He had found the highest pursuit in life, he was never more to leave it till the final word was spoken.

And now we will turn to our diary, for we are prepared for it. The silent, unpretending writer was herself touched by the spirit which passes before us in its triumphal feats, which gives to these private extracts, insignificant in themselves, an interest to those who sympathise with the inward life of humanity, and know that only with such spirit-working is history made, that is to say, the progress of the race advanced.

CHAPTER III.

CONFESSIONS.

WE now come to the written testimony of the young lady herself. Almost on the very first page we read of the effect produced by the personal acquaintance of the great musician on her heart, when he was a somewhat deaf hypochondriac of five-and-forty years.

On the 30th of January, she writes:—

"All day long I have been occupied with Beethoven, that is to say, with the expectation of the arrival of his nephew, till I am quite ashamed of myself; all the more so because I do not find Nanni's and Leopold's idea so absurd as many might. I can neither wish it nor give it up; and I am unable to believe that my veneration for his genius will be lessened by a nearer acquaintance with the man. My esteem for him must increase, if I find him half as genial and kind-hearted as he has been represented to us to be, and which, in my eyes, only renders him more than commonly interesting."

It is worthy of note how unconsciously the inward conviction of the man's true worth finds vent in these few words, and with what confidence she expresses her belief that the world's opinion of the highly gifted musician is correct. For, instinctively, she recognises the worth of the man beneath the surface of the artist.

Ere this, Beethoven had written to her father to say that he would himself bring his nephew.

To the right understanding of this arrangement, we must remark in explanation that the lad's mother, who was an intriguing, haughty person, irritated at her maternal rights being interfered with, and her power over her son transferred to his guardian, avenged herself on Beethoven by doing all in her power to render his life a burden. Constant disputes arose about the property which she, as the daughter of a wealthy burgher of Vienna, had brought to her husband as her marriage portion, and to which the boy Karl was sole heir. But what tried Beethoven more than aught else was the means she adopted for gaining access to the lad, once even dressing herself up in men's clothes, and, under this disguise, obtaining admittance to the playground of the Institute and mixing amongst the boys. Expecting great things from the lad, and hoping that "his name, through his nephew, would become doubly illustrious," Beethoven naturally feared the result of this "bad woman's" influence over her son, whom she instigated to lying, deception, and dissimulation of every kind towards his uncle. We shall hear more of this as we go on with the diary. Unfortunately, we are compelled to recognise that the too high standard he had formed of his nephew's future, clashing with his sensitive horror of and severity towards the mother, tended to bring about a result the very reverse of his intentions. A bad education, a moral depravity, and a corruption of manners were the lot of the unlucky child.

Beethoven's letter ran as follows:—

"I announce to you, with great pleasure, that at last, to-morrow, I shall bring you my dear ward entrusted to my care. For the rest, I must beg you again to allow his mother no influence over him, no matter how or when she sees him. But I will speak more fully on this subject with you to-morrow. You will have to keep a watch on your servants, for mine was corrupted by *her* soon enough, although for another purpose. I will tell you more in detail by word of mouth, though I should much prefer silence on the subject. Still, for the sake of your future cosmopolitan position, I must make these sad communications."

Then the young lady writes on a fresh page, without any date:—

"It is quite impossible for me to think of anything but the agreeable emotions resulting from our interesting acquaintance with Beethoven. He passed the whole evening with mother and me, and during that time proved to us that he is moved by such rare high moral principles, and is such a noble estimable man, that my enthusiasm for him is in every way increased."

The rest of the page is left open to be filled in at a more convenient time, but the impressions of the next few days seem to have found no leisure for a closer description of this first quiet meeting. The next record is dated the 22nd of February, after which we will let the extracts speak for themselves, in the order in which they come, merely adding the necessary explanations and supplements from Beethoven's own letters, to render the diary complete. Many trifling incidents are related, of course, referring to the domestic life, and observations and feelings of a reserved woman's mind. Still, that she herself was not always certain of her own impressions, though she put them to paper, trusting very often to her intuitive perceptions instead, proves the correctness of what we have already remarked, that her education and talents were of a high order, as we shall see by her observations on life, and men, and on Beethoven himself in particular.

In general, however, the tone of these extracts is that of a simple, well-educated, refined woman who describes things as she finds them.

The next extract is as follows:—

"A few words on yesterday evening's conversation. Beethoven's appearance pleases me greatly. More I cannot say, as I hardly spoke to him. The day before yesterday he was with us in the evening and won all our hearts. The modesty and heartiness of his disposition please us extremely! The sorrow which his unhappy connection with the boy's mother entails preys upon his spirits. It afflicts me too, for *he* is a man who ought to be happy. May he attach himself to us, and by our warm sympathy and interest find peace and serenity!

"On father asking him why he left us so early when the children were present, he answered that 'his face was not in harmony with happy faces, and he felt so conscious of the fact that he could not bear it any longer!'

"I fear me greatly that when I come to know this noble excellent man more intimately, my feelings for him will deepen into something warmer than friendship, and that then I shall have many unhappy hours before me. But I will endure anything, provided only I have it in my power to make his life brighter. To Duncker, I shall often write. All my affairs interest him!"

"*February* 23rd.—Beethoven was with us again yesterday evening. Nanni was at the rehearsal, so mamma and I were alone. While mamma was out of the room, intent on the comforts of the boy, I spoke with Beethoven on the subject of his compositions and music, which interested me as much as possible, for I was enabled to observe his character at the same time. It is not an easy matter for me to talk much to him, and although in consequence of his misfortune general conversation is difficult, yet I always manage to make others join if I can."

"*February* 26*th.*—The day before yesterday, Beethoven was with us for several hours in the evening. A very pleasant impression of this evening was left on my memory, making me wish to enjoy many more like it. He showed us himself, or rather allowed us to see in him the goodness of heart which is his special characteristic. Whether he spoke of his friends, or of his excellent mother, or gave his opinion on those who are contemporaries in art with himself, he proved to us that his heart is as well cultivated as his head. In fact, for my part, I find all his observations so just, and of such sterling merit, that I think they ought to be preserved in writing. How delighted I shall be if he continues to enjoy our circle!"

"*March* 2*nd.*—Is that true? I cried out, after a conversation with Nanni on Beethoven. Has he already become so dear to me that my sister's laughing advice, not to fall in love with him, pains and troubles me beyond measure? Poor me! I will not allow myself to dwell on such thoughts, though after all a life devoted to loving, even if it entails a few sorrowful hours, is better, far better, than to let one's warm heart vegetate in an empty deathlike monotony. It is not true now! Yet, when I know him better, he must become dear, *very dear* to me. He can and may be that; why then think about a closer union which common sense tells me is impossible?

"How can I be so vain as to believe or imagine that the power of captivating such a soul as his is reserved to me? Such a genius! and *such a heart!* Ah, indeed! a noble heart like his is exactly according to my longings. But no more on this subject for many a long day, or all ease in his presence will vanish. I am glad that beyond a wee bit of fun, I have never spoken seriously with Nanni on the subject."

"*March 4th.*—Beethoven's present, the 'Schlacht bei Vittoria,' gave me great pleasure, all the more so as it is a proof that he thinks of us. This morning I was not in very bright spirits, mamma's constant cough during the night worried me; how could I help then the tears running down my cheeks when Karl read aloud to me, while I was making breakfast, a letter which he had received from his noble uncle? To-day I am not happy, decidedly; and—*and he is not as happy as he ought to be!*"

"*March 7th.*—Yesterday evening I was carried into a state of ecstasy by the music, and under its charming influence enabled to forget for a time the thousand small vexations which earlier in the day had put me in a disagreeable humour. I was overjoyed, too, to notice that many of my neighbours shared a similar influence. Beethoven listened for a while. If only this trouble with Karl's mother were at an end! The poor man takes it so much to heart that he will, I fear, be ill. I have written much about Beethoven to Duncker. How I wish he would answer me!"

With respect to the guardianship and law processes which played so prominent a part in the great musician's life, the following letter, addressed by him to Father Giannatasio, will find a fitting place here.

" In seeing the mother, I must beg that you do

not leave her with him; explain to her that he is too busy; no one can know and judge better than I do on this point. All my preconceived plans for the lad's welfare will be upset if you do. I wish I were not so anxious on this head—the burden is heavy enough as it is. I gathered from my conversation yesterday with the solicitor that a year and a day may dawdle on before we can know what really does belong to the child. Ought I to have added to this trial the trouble which I hoped to have avoided by means of your Institute?"

Thus he seems to have begun to lose confidence in the Institute. The lady continues:—

"*March* 11*th*.—Yesterday I was not pleased, not quite satisfied with the concert, in spite of the enjoyment I always receive in listening to music—music *composed by our beloved Beethoven*. He has been very dear to me lately! His conversation is so embued with true deep feeling! I hope he will come often, and attach himself truly to us!"

To explain the above extract, we will quote a

paragraph which appeared in the Leipzig *Allgemeine Musik-Zeitung*:—

"Violin concert by Beethoven. The performer failed. The overture to 'Egmont,' incomparably played."

The defective manner in which Beethoven's music was generally performed at that time was one of the reasons for his not being on very good terms with Vienna (otherwise a very musical town), and for his wish to visit England, where he had often been invited.

The young lady writes further:—

"*March 12th.*—For a long time yesterday evening, I hoped in vain that Beethoven would come. Mamma and I were the only two at home, only a few of our usual visitors came. At last, just as I had settled down into the usual evening's work, some one rang, and, behold, it was our dear friend at last! He has no idea, I think, how fond we all are of him, I in particular. He never struck me as an ugly man, but lately his face pleases me, his manners too are so original, and all he says has weight."

Beethoven could not possibly be called a handsome man. His somewhat flat, broad nose, and rather wide mouth, his small piercing eyes and swarthy complexion, pock-marked into the bargain, gave him a strong resemblance to a mulatto, and caused many young ladies to pronounce him "ugly." But an artist who took his portrait that year, describes him thus :—

"Beethoven has an earnest grave expression, and usually his quick piercing eyes glance upwards with a gloomy look. His lips are closed, but the mouth is not unpleasant in expression." The same artist, Professor Klöber, well known as the painter of the curtain representing the 'Triumph of Galatea' in the Berlin Opera House, describes Beethoven's personal appearance as follows :—

"He wore a light blue frock coat with yellow buttons, with white waistcoat and neckcloth as was the fashion then, but his clothes looked untidy. His hair was of a bluish steel colour, black slightly turning grey. His eyes were a bluish grey and very lively. When his hair was uncombed, or in disarray, he looked veritably demoniacal."

Another acquaintance, A. Schindler, says of him, "At times he looked like a Jupiter." This impression must have arisen from his grand, magnificent forehead, surmounted by rich curling locks like a Zeus's head. An anecdote was circulated in Vienna about him to the effect that, one evening, in a drawing-room full of people, a lady praised the musician's grand brow in glowing terms. Beethoven heard her remarks, and, not insensible of their merits, boldly said, "Very well, then, kiss my forehead!" and the charming woman rewarded his boldness by kissing his brow on the spot. This lady was no other than Maximiliane Brentano, of Frankfort on the Main, who told the story herself later on, and to whom Beethoven dedicated, in 1821, his exquisite Sonata in E sharp, op. 109.

The diary goes on :—

"*March* 14*th*.—Beethoven was with us again last evening. Mamma, Nanni and Leopold, conversed with him through me. What a pity! But how willingly I would undertake the office for ever! He was in a very good humour, possibly because his guardianship affairs are happily ended. We talked a great deal about our musical society union, and laughed and jested merrily over the regulations in our town," &c.

In explanation of the following extract, we must add here that the now celebrated Amateur Musical Society (Gesellschaft der Musikfreunde), which had been founded a year or two previously in Vienna, was generally spoken of by Beethoven as the "Society of Music's Murderers," in consequence of the small amount of artistic merit to be found in the dilettante performances of the members when first the society was formed. His opinion of the political and other public institutions of Austria is well known. Besides, he had good grounds for fault-finding, and for the scorn he expressed for these things by his experiences during the tedious lawsuit connected with his guardianship.

Just about this period he wrote to the father of the young lady, F. A. Brentano, in Frankfort, that "our government is proving day by day how it wants governing." He alternately made fun of and abused the then existing "Wienervölkchen," whom he characterised by the words of the "noble sufferer," in his favourite and oft-quoted Odyssey :—

"There were seated the leaders of the Phœnicians,
Drinking and eating, for such was their wont year by year."*

The young lady continues in the same extract :—

"It delighted me to know that he has read Leopold's (her brother-in-law Schmerling) verses, for now he can recognise and understand in what honour we hold him. When Leopold was going, he was for leaving us also, but Nanni observed to him that he would be conferring a great kindness on us if he stayed, to which he replied 'that he ought not, considering he was our latest acquaintance.' But we reassured him by saying that we did not approve of such

* Book vii. lines 98, 99.

formal etiquette with him. And he stayed. How delighted I should be if he grew fond of us! If he only would attach himself to our family! Duncker the same. Will it really come to pass?"

"*March* 17*th.*—The day before yesterday Beethoven was with us the whole evening. In the afternoon he had been gathering violets for us, as he said himself, to bring spring to us. This remembrance of us gave me great pleasure. I spoke with him about walks, baths (the baths near Vienna), and Karl's mother. His pure, unspoiled admiration for nature is very beautiful! His confession of distrust, that he doubted many of the coinciding circumstances, as also the name of Schönauer, which made us anxious a short while ago, amused us exceedingly last night. Nanni had just returned from the rehearsal."

It may be as well to state here that the advocate employed by his ward's mother, as also the "kind harmless uncle" of the lady, bore the name of Schönauer, and by means of his legal science assisted the boy's mother in her intrigues, thus bringing a great deal of sorrow and trouble on the helpless, unworldly musician.

The diary continues :—

"I was often alone with him, and feared he might grow weary; but if he had, he could very easily have left us. When father came in, we entreated him so warmly to remain and take supper with us that he consented, and we intensely enjoyed listening to his rich, original remarks and puns. He gave us also many decided proofs that he is beginning to have confidence in us. He did not leave till nearly twelve o'clock. I would willingly give up my sleep for this to happen often."

Evidently Beethoven unfolded in the bosom of this family, where he had placed his beloved "son," and where he felt quite at home himself, all the hitherto pent-up riches of his warm, well-stored heart and mind. Hence it is not to be wondered at that the earnest manliness of his nature should have made a deep impression on this young lady's *heart*. She writes further :—

"*Thursday, March* 21*st.*—I have been eager to get to my diary, because I have not dared even to tell my sister all that has been passing in my mind since this morning; and she, hitherto, has shared my every thought. Can I conceal from myself that which makes me long to weep continually? Yes; it must be confessed, Beethoven interests me to the selfish point of desiring, nay, longing, that I, and *I* alone, may please him! When father repeated his remark, made in reference to a contemplated journey (to London), that he would never be able to form a closer tie than the one which bound him now to his nephew, then the thought that we should be separated from him gave rise to the idea—for what else can I call it?—which has been troubling me all day, and put me in this state of longing to weep my eyes out.

"I am deeply ashamed to make this confession, but let the one judge me who, with *a heart capable of untold powers of loving*, has already begun to understand that these exquisite feelings must be pent-up within oneself. And that in spite of the inward conviction that this great love would make the loved one happy, if it dared to find expression, yet it *must* be hidden away out of sight, and suppressed!

"I have been asking myself lately the same question which I did formerly: Why it is impossible to be satisfied with childish and sisterly affection? Speculate as one may on the subject, it is of no use: all one can do is to become master of one's own emotions, unfortunately a hard task hitherto for me. Until I have attained this mastery over myself, and so gained peace, I will try and think less of my future on this subject, or rather promise myself that I will wait with childlike patience, and in the meantime continue to live as a true and faithful daughter, sister, and friend. In this manner I shall live on till the time comes when it will not be such a hard matter to overcome the deep, but unreasonable longings of my heart, and enjoy peace. A little hope will thus brighten my existence, without which peace will never come. So I will hope on! It is a pity that I must never forget, but always remember that, hope as I may, no certainty, no belief, can be mixed up with it! I know I have written much that I ought not even to think about, but my feelings are so intense!"

"*March* 23rd.—When I returned home, I found that Beethoven had passed the whole evening there. He had brought Shakespeare with him, and played with mother and the children at ninepins. He told them a great deal about his parents, as also of his grandfather, who must have been a true and honourable man."

This conversation of Beethoven's, which, if written down, would have given us important information concerning his youth, unfortunately has not been preserved in the reminiscences of the lady. One fact alone she considers worthy of record on this head. "Once he told us," she says, "he was educated with proverbs, for his tutor was a Jesuit." Thus he, as well as his great predecessor, Gluck, had narrow-minded discipline and doctrine to struggle against in the development of their free thoughts and genius. This is a very noteworthy fact to be taken into consideration when judging his genius.

The young lady goes on as follows with her confessions :—

"*March* 30*th*.—All yesterday, and for several previous evenings, we expected Beethoven, but we expected in vain. Father suggested taking me and the little one to fetch him. I refused, and thereby deprived myself of a veritable joy. Something within told me that I ought not to go, and when father returned home, he said I had done quite right. The dear man has not been well the last few days. Everything concerning him interests me deeply, but I am easily put in a bad humour lately."

"*April* 3*rd*.—We have only seen our dear Beethoven once for a few moments in company with the Schönauers, but yesterday he wrote to his little nephew such a charming letter, so full of kind and good things, that it was a real pleasure to read it. I do not, however, think it is quite right of him to disturb the child's present state of ingenuous ignorance, by placing a confidence in him which he is not old enough to appreciate, and which may have the effect of making him ponder over things he cannot understand. Or, perhaps, as he is not naturally truthful, it may lead him to indulge in falsehood. But this may be the result of dear Beethoven's wish to compensate the lad for a mother's love by his own great love, and to be all in all to him."

We must interrupt the young lady here, to enable us to judge clearly of these events, and that no misunderstanding may occur later on. Fanny's remark respecting Beethoven's treatment of his nephew is of the highest importance, if we wish thoroughly to understand the unhappy relations which were so bitter in their after consequences. Hence, we shall only remark here that it was owing to this very intense love, and the exaggerated expectations he formed, both morally and intellectually, of the lad's future, which had brought about the sad series of disasters which ultimately ended in the terrible attempt at suicide, an event which was only too closely connected with Beethoven's early death. It was his affection for the boy which led him so constantly to visit at the Giannatasio's house. In other respects, he could not find there the food his mental wants required, and perhaps this was unfortunately the reason why he unjustly judged and condemned the mistake later on.

The young lady continues:—

"*April* 11*th*.—Tuesday afternoon. I saw Beethoven again, for the first time since he has been suffering from the illness we feared was hanging over him. At first I was quite alone with him, but as nothing I said seemed to interest him, I began to feel discouraged. Presently Leopold, Nanni, and mother came in, and then he brightened up. In referring to his late illness, he remarked that one of those attacks of cholic would carry him off some day; upon which I said that that must not happen for many a long year yet, and he replied, 'He is a bad man who does not know how to die! I knew it when a lad of fifteen.' Thinking that he meant that he had not done much for his art, I cried out impulsively, 'Then you may die fearlessly!' These few words distressed me greatly; the thought arose he might die early."

Here, again, we interrupt the young lady to add that in the extracts supplied from memory she observes, in reference to the above conversation, that "he answered again as if to himself, 'I have other things to think about first.'" We shall soon learn in what these "other things" consisted.

The young lady finishes with :—

"His new composition from Tiedge's *Urania*, 'Die Hoffnung' (Hope), with its accompanying recitative, is simply divine. I and Nanni were both delighted with it; it carried us up into heaven!"

HOPE.
From the German of Tiedge.

"Does God exist? and will He e'er fulfil
That which the bleeding heart doth long for and await?
Or will this most mysterious Being Himself reveal
At the last judgment of the quick and dead?
Man must not, dare not, question, but hope on still!

"Thou who dost love to sanctify the calm pure night,
 By soft and tender veiling of all the grief
 Which on some weary laden soul hath cast its blight,
 O Hope, in thee may every sufferer find relief;
 May feel himself uplifted to the glorious height
 Where angels, counting all his tears, give solace brief!

"When memory alone is left to mourn the past,
 And when beneath dead branches of the bygone days
 She sits, to think of tones whose echoes may not last,
 Oh, then approach, and, shadowed by the darkness, gaze
 Upon the cheerless one, who low himself hath cast
 Upon the deep sunk tombs, and there in memory stays.

"Should he complain, and, looking up to heaven,
 Bemoan his fate, as those last fading rays of light decline
 Upon his dying day? O Hope, do not deny,
 But grant that round his cloud a brilliant line
 Of glorious light may greet his grief-dimmed sorrowing eye,
 That, in a dying sunset, his last cloud may shine!"

Already in the year 1811, Beethoven wrote to the author of *Urania*, after he had been with him in Teplitz, " You met me with the brotherly greeting of 'Thou'; * so let it be, my Tiedge! Short as was our acquaintance, we soon learned to know each other, and to have no reserve one

---

* In Germany the familiar style of address between relations and dear friends is 'Thou' instead of 'you.'

with the other." Inviolable faith in a "happiness which never wavered" was the bond which bound these two together, and as Tiedge's poetry, in spite of the extravagance of its metaphors, made a deep impression on the musician's heart, he was enabled to give depth and intensity to his composition, and render it like a sigh of yearning as of one in pain—Oh for hope! The more so, perhaps, because he was deprived of the enjoyment of many external pleasures, and had never known happiness in any form but that of *music.*

The diary goes on:—

"*April* 20*th*.—In the evening our dear Beethoven came to us. He said many bright and kind things, but there was not much conversation. He has a bantering, teasing manner, in which he displays as much originality and ingenuity as he does in his music. I wish he would come oftener, that the slight stiffness and formality of his visits might wear off—I mean that then one could talk to him just as one thinks."

About this time, clouds began to gather on his horizon. The young lady writes:—

"*May 4th.*—A few words on my miserable frame of mind yesterday, only kept in check by constant and almost restless activity. It was about this time last year that I lost my betrothed, and the remembrance of my sorrow still makes me feel sad. Also, I miss Duncker's sympathy terribly; we have not heard from him for so long; added to which, Beethoven's manner towards us has altered. He is cold now for the first time, and I find myself grieving over it, no matter how I am occupied. The fear that he may withdraw his treasure from under our care follows me constantly, since I asked the boy why he had been crying, and he replied that his uncle had forbidden him to tell. At first Nanni and I thought the cause of vexation might be the length of time which had elapsed since he received a letter, but we found out we were wrong in our surmises. God only knows what it all means, but I know how painfully I shall feel it if the link which binds us to the noblest of men is snapped, as suddenly as it was formed."

The cause for Beethoven's ill-humour at this special time is not at all clear, unless it arose from a feeling of dissatisfaction regarding the Institute, which did not come up to the high standard he considered necessary to the development of the boy's talents, the depth and extent of which he sadly exaggerated in his own mind. He began to speak of the school as "bad," "stupid," "wanting in backbone," &c. &c. And these doubts as to the worth of the Institute not only caused him many unhappy hours, and often robbed him of his peace of mind, but brought about many disagreeables, and at last an open rupture. He tormented himself and the family with constant complaints, till his relations with them were first undermined, and then finally snapped asunder. We shall see this for ourselves as we go on.

The young lady's remarks on the great master's "ways" are worthy of notice.

"*May 8th.*—Our position with Beethoven is beginning to make me anxious, and robs me of the pleasure I took in him, not only as a man, but as a master in his art; for if he really has a charge to make against us, my high opinion of his character will be modified."

"*May 27th.*—He was with us the evening before last, but his conduct is at times so very moody and unfriendly that I feel shy with him, and dare not venture to be on the intimate terms that we all so much enjoyed in the winter. Circumstances are in fault, I have no doubt; but the hope I once indulged in, that Beethoven might become our devoted friend, can scarcely be realised now that he cools towards us at the very first misunderstanding."

"*June 7th.*—An evening or two ago Beethoven came to us. Many of his observations made me long to cry out, 'Yes, it is so, for that is how *I* feel!' But I had no sympathy with one remark to the effect that *his life was of no worth to himself, he only wished to live for the boy's sake!* These two expressions moved me to such a degree that I burst into tears. The earnest longing of my heart for us to be more to Beethoven than ordinary friends, and for him to attach himself to our circle, is gradually losing force, and Nanni agrees with me that it is useless to hope for it. I have written to Duncker on the subject."

"*June* 29*th*.—During the time I was laid aside with suffering, Beethoven came to see me twice, and intensely I enjoyed his visits. Perhaps it was the difficulty I had in speaking to him, owing to my weakness, or rather the awkwardness of expressing my thoughts through another person's lips, which brought about a fit of depression and increased the fever. Even if it were so, I would willingly suffer the same over and over again in order to have the pleasure of hearing such a highly gifted, interesting, frank-minded man talk. He is far above ordinary mortals, and too sensitive in soul to mix with the world. His devotion to and admiration for truth and goodness have lost none of their intensity through his experience of life, although times out of count lately he must have been tempted to forsake both.

"The history of his rupture with Lichnowsky, and the history of his lawsuit, are not very enlivening; still, as they concern him, they naturally interest me exceedingly; the former especially, as it proved the great decision of his character."

The young lady describes as follows Beethoven's rupture with his oldest Vienna friend and patron, Prince Karl Lichnowsky: "One evening during the invasion of the French, many of whom were guests in the Prince's house, Beethoven was entreated to play on the piano. He refused to comply with the Prince's desire, whereupon his host tried to compel him, and a scene followed, which Beethoven cut short by abruptly quitting the house." This happened in the autumn of 1806, at Lichnowsky's place, near Grätz, in Silesia. A reconciliation took place a few years later.

The "history of his lawsuit" is as follows.

In the year 1808, Beethoven accepted the appointment of Kapellmeister to merry king Jérôme of Westphalia, and was to receive a stipulated sum yearly from the three Austrian princes together. That is to say, the Archduke Rudolph and Princes Kinsky and Lobkowitz agreed to pay him a certain sum yearly, for the remainder of his life. But, in consequence of the Austrian state becoming bankrupt a couple of years afterwards, Beethoven's income was reduced to a fifth part. After several tedious processes to get back the money, during which Kinsky suddenly died and Lobkowitz failed, Beethoven's income increased sufficiently in 1816 for him to meet the expenses of his nephew's education.

The young lady continues :—

"He was not in such good spirits as last time, and although he warmed up while relating various episodes of his past life, and while dissecting others, which forced me to exclaim, 'But human nature is frail!' he did not appear to get brighter or happier. I was sorry he was so low-spirited, for nothing would give me greater pleasure than for him to feel cheered and amused in our society. I hardly hope now that he will ever do so."

We will add here that the Vienna Congress of 1814 had a very injurious moral effect on the town and surrounding country, through the presence of numerous foreigners and certain rich people who dissipated their money after a fashion that in itself was calculated to do an immense deal of harm. Beethoven personally became aware of this sad change, by the demoralised state of his servants.

The diary goes on :—

"How I would delight to hear him play! Over and over again I have intimated this to him, without exactly asking him to fulfil my wish, but he has never offered to give me the pleasure. I scarcely dare allow myself to judge whether this arises from exaggerated modesty, which prevents his perceiving the intense amount of delight and pleasure we should derive from such an act of kindness on his part; or if he has such a very exalted opinion of his own worth and merit that he imagines we should not be able to appreciate to the full his wondrous playing. If the latter, surely it must be the result of pride! Perhaps, in his place, I might think the same, but if I did, I would be more amiable."

We will here remark that this aversion of Beethoven's to "play in society" manifested itself very early in life. It was, as it were, a part of his inner life which prevented his overcoming the shy reserve habitual to him, even when it related to the art he loved so well.

The young lady continues:—

"The couple of days I was convalescent, I employed in writing to our dear faithful friend, Duncker. I had leisure and quiet for the task, but agreeable and pleasant as it is to write to him, I cannot tell him of all I think. My thoughts would not flow from my pen as quickly as I might have wished. I knew then that frequently I must have forced myself not to be too interested in Beethoven, a state of things that in my uneventful life was very apt to happen, and the result of which would be, if not a miserable existence, at least a less peaceful one than has been my lot since my last year's trouble.

"I long with a great longing for a closer friendship with this man, thereby putting aside and crushing out of my existence those other feelings which have crept into my heart, enabling me to enjoy a sympathetic intercourse with our dear friend, in lieu of the other joys debarred to me. But he must, in his way, be to us as Duncker is. Perhaps I am expecting too much, but the latter wish is genuine, for what is more lasting and more lovely in this world than the enjoyment of a true friendship?"

A bitter blow followed upon this fresh outburst of the deep emotions of her heart, in the shape of the first real disturbing cause to the friendship between Beethoven and the family.

"*July* 29*th*.—Rain followed our sunshine, or rather a thunder-clap seemed to have fallen over us, when, on reaching home, we found Beethoven's letter with its enclosure from Karl's mother.

Pained as I felt when I had read it, it nevertheless consoled me, for mamma's words, 'he has given us warning,' together with the mother's disgraceful letter, made me fear that some misunderstanding had taken place. During several hours the thought that we must give up the friendship of him who has daily grown dearer and dearer to me distressed me exceedingly. To-day I feel it less bitterly, especially when I remember that his letter is certainly friendly in tone, and that he evidently is kindly disposed towards us.

"I will not trust myself to give an opinion on his mode of proceeding in this affair; he says himself that weighty reasons have induced him to take this step. Who knows if the great anxiety the child's future welfare causes him, an anxiety that no one can reproach him for, not even the mother, will be good for the boy in the end? I can't say. Perhaps he fears being reproached with not taking care of the boy himself. I have fancied at times that he shrinks from any such imputation being cast on him, much as he tries to hide it. I feel very sorry for him, for I am convinced that this step will do harm to Karl.

"Then, again, I regret this step because many people will blame him for it, and those who do not will be hostile to our Institute, and that again will bring trouble. I have one hope left, and that is that papa's answer will make him change his mind, though I scarcely know if it would be wise to wish it may, for if by any chance anything should go wrong with the boy, we should be blamed. I consider him a just man too. How truly and gratefully he speaks of the motherly care the boy has had while with us. I know of no event which has so pained me as this one has!"

The letter dated the 28th of July 1816 not only gives Beethoven's reasons for acting as he did in this affair, but shows how faulty he could be. And also it is very noticeable how, in spite of her intrigues against the 'Zauberflöte,' he calls her the "queen of night," and likens himself, as the boy's protector, to Sarastro.

The letter is as follows:—

"Dear Friend,—Many circumstances oblige me to have Karl with me. Not, I can assure you, from any drawback either in you or your excellent Institute, but simply because I think it will be to the boy's advantage. It is a trial, and I shall beg you to help me with your advice, as also to allow Karl to visit your Institute from time to time. We will always be grateful to you, and never be able to forget all the kindness and care your excellent wife has bestowed on the lad. I would send you four times as much as I now enclose, if I could afford it. In the meanwhile, if ever I have the opportunity, I will gratefully do everything in my power to further the interests of your Institute, by making known the physical and moral good you have done to Karl.

"As regards the appearance of the 'queen of night,' that must be as it has been hitherto, especially if Karl is operated upon in your house. He will naturally not feel very well for a few days, and as he will be more sensitive and irritable at that time, it will be as well not to leave her with him, for fear those impressions should be deepened which we would rather were not renewed. The enclosed scrawl will prove to you how little we may depend upon her tact and good intentions, and also will show you how right I was at one time to be on my guard against her. This time I have answered her not as a Sarastro, but as a Sultan.

"Say everything that is kind for me to your dear children and excellent wife. I leave Vienna to-morrow morning at five, but I shall often come in from the baths.

"As always, faithfully yours,
"L. v. BEETHOVEN."

About this same period Beethoven had spoken to a young friend of his from Courland, a Dr. Bursy, about the school, and complained of its shortcomings, regretting he had sent the boy there. "Karl must become an artist or scholar in order to live a high life," he said on that occasion—and to this end he now determined to take the boy to himself and let him share the "high life" he lived in. And what else did this elderly, partially deaf man possess in the world, besides his gifted nephew?

The young lady thoroughly understood this state of feeling, for she writes on the 1st of August:—

"Beethoven's friend, Herr Bernard, came this evening and assured us that the mother's letters had nothing at all to do with the boy being taken away from us, and that Beethoven always spoke of our house with gratitude. I believe that the reason he did it was to have the boy entirely to himself, for he certainly loves him passionately, and no wonder, considering Karl is the only being in the world who entirely belongs to him. Still, I can't help wishing for the boy's sake that he could remain with us; it would be better for him than living with his uncle, as the latter will find out, perhaps, when it is too late."

August 16th she writes:—"I was not in good spirits for going out (in society) to-day, as father had made me feel very unhappy about our beloved Beethoven. He thinks he will not be here long, for he is far too sensitive, and feels things too acutely in his delicate state of health to be able to bear up against troubles much longer."

Father Giannatasio's presentiments respecting the great master were only too well realised, and the after experiences with his nephew coincided strangely with these lugubrious prophecies. And the young lady was right, also, when she prophesied that sorrow would follow Karl's removal from her father's house. She writes:—

"It is very consoling to me certainly to learn that he has nothing to complain of against us, while at the same time I grieve terribly at Karl's departure, because I *feel sure* it would have been better for his sake if he had remained with us. Then again I think to myself how pleasant it will be for Beethoven to have the only one being constantly with him on whom he has the right to lean. Still I am anxious about it, for I fear that the very intensity of this pleasure will keep Beethoven from being as strict with the thoughtless boy as will be necessary, if he wishes him to be a comfort to him in after years. I think it is scarcely possible for another human being on the face of the earth to so earnestly desire the happiness of this noble man as I do. And yet I fear that my wish and desire will never be realised. I must try and be satisfied if it is so, even to a slight extent."

On the 29th of August the young lady makes some reference to Beethoven's lament at his want of means—a state of things that unfortunately was only too true. Since he had taken his nephew to live with him, his expenses had increased considerably, and, with all his hard work to meet the demands on his purse, his income by no means augmented in proportion. And no doubt one of the chief causes for his wearing out so soon arose from the fact of his being obliged to earn sufficient for daily necessities, at a time when his health was failing, and he was getting into years. The young lady writes:—

"A few days ago Beethoven returned from the baths, grumbling, as usual, over his expenses. When I saw him, and heard him speak so kindly of us, the wish of my heart again asserted itself that he would attach himself to us; also that he *knew* how *very* fond we are of him. He seems quite well, and says that he knows he shall be strong enough soon, his constitution is so healthy."

On the 13th of September, the young lady refers to a subject which later on became only too significant.

"Yesterday I passed such an intensely interesting day with Beethoven at the baths that it will require several days to elapse before I regain possession of my usual quiet state of mind. Everything I heard and noticed about him interested me so much that I willingly narrate it here circumstantially, although I know that it would be impossible for me ever to forget the least little incident connected with such an eventful day. The knowledge of whom we were going to see, and the looking forward to a day fine and lovely enough for our promised expedition, both tended to put me in a state of happy excitement. But when it arrived, it was not quite so pleasant as we had anticipated; for, as most probably Beethoven had given up the hope of seeing us, we found him up to his ears in work, and so absent that the conviction was forced upon us that we were in his way."

Here is the elucidation of the remark, "I have other things to think about," already referred to. In a rough-book belonging to Beethoven, dating this summer of 1816, there is a sketch of his great sonata, op. 106, the "Symphony in D," as the great musician himself terms the first and second movements in his Ninth Symphony, besides "Preludes to my Masses:" hence it was not to be wondered at that he should be "absent" when called upon to entertain unexpected visitors. He was then working on the greatest of his works. The young lady continues:—

"When we reached home from the hotel, our fatigue was forgotten, we were so distressed at

Beethoven's bad humour caused by his servant's stupidity. I was excessively grieved that we were the unwitting means of making him feel so wretched. However, he soon got over it, and on leaving us cried out that we must not swear at him if anything went wrong. I was glad to see him all right again."

Then, again, on the 16th of September, she refers to several slight incidents:—

"A few words more on our stay at the baths. The great interest we take in all connected with Beethoven tempted us to indulge our curiosity to an extent that was really culpable, although I think that it would have been beyond human power to have resisted such a temptation. Placed as we were in a room filled with associations of his beloved art, and surrounded as we were with the indications of his daily life, how could we help wishing to examine every object that spoke to us of him? Nanni found a memorandum book which appeared to contain many significant things."

Again we will interrupt the young lady to

observe that no doubt this was a skeleton of the speech that was to be delivered at the approaching Beethoven Festival. The young lady remembered afterwards having seen on a stained piece of paper the words: "My heart overflows at the sight of lovely nature—although without her." She says this gave her much to think about.

Her diary continues:—

"How bitterly we were punished for our curiosity when I made the painful discovery that he must often be *very, very* unhappy! The child-like faith, and high inspiration, which is truly *divine*, not only delighted us, but awoke our sympathy and respect to a degree that, with me at least, is almost beyond expression. It was not right of us to have looked into the book, but having done so, it gave us the opportunity of acknowledging that this noble man is more worthy of admiration and esteem than we had hitherto been able to judge. I was very much overcome, and for long after I was in bed I could not sleep—but at last nature asserted her rights, and I slept."

We will quote here one extract from the book above referred to :—

"Do I watch Karl as if he were my own son? Every weakness, every trifle even tending to this great end. It is a hard matter for me. But He above is there! Without Him is nothing!"

The young lady continues :—

"The scene the next morning with the servant horrified us. Our indignation at such disgraceful conduct, and sorrow that Beethoven must live with such a wretched person, knew no bounds. I especially felt quite upset with the affair. However, it soon passed over; and when he followed us to the Anton Bridge to breakfast with us, and told us all about the scene, he apologised for his passion and anger, and warned Karl *not to act like his uncle.*"

The young lady relates the event from memory. She says : "Beethoven appeared with a scratched face, and explained that he had had a scene with his servant, who is leaving. 'Look,' said he, 'how he has marked me,' and then he went on to tell us that, although this man knew that he was deaf, he would take no trouble to make his master hear."

The narration goes on in a manner that calls for our especial attention.

"Presently a very animated and interesting conversation began between father and Beethoven. It arose from a remark of my father's to the effect that, as our poor friend led such a very miserable existence with this individual, whom there seemed no hope of improving, it would be best for him to find a wife who would attend to all those numberless offices his sad state of deafness required, with a patience and devotion impossible to expect from any one else. My father went on to ask him if he did not know of any one likely to suit him. I listened from my corner with the most intense and painful excitement, while he confessed to what I had long since feared in my heart, that he loved in vain! Five years ago he made the acquaintance of a lady, whom to marry would have been the highest happiness life could have afforded him.

It was not to be thought of; was quite impossible, in fact, and was a chimera. But still his feelings remain the same now as then. 'I cannot put her out of my thoughts,' were words which pained and hurt me beyond measure.

"He loves still! this clears up for me the meaning of those few words I found on the bit of paper."

That we on our side may fully understand the episode itself, to which Beethoven thus refers in his unexpected confession, and the influence it had on his inner life, we must interrupt the young lady's narrative for a time, while we take a retrospect of the great musician's past, and penetrate into the deepest mysteries of a human being's soul.

CHAPTER IV.

LOVE EPISODES.

WE will begin by quoting from the original a simple, but very matter of fact communication, made by Doctor Wegeler, Beethoven's Bonn friend, in answer to a statement made by a Vienna acquaintance of many years' standing, that Beethoven "was never married, and what was more marvellous still, never had any love passages in his life."

He says:—

"The truth is, Beethoven was always in love, and generally with some lady of high rank. Fräulein Jeanette d'Honrath of Cologne, was his first love, as also that of his young Bonn friend, Stephan von Breuning. She once visited Bonn, and stayed with the Breuning family. She was a beautiful fair girl, of a bright merry disposition, pleasing manners, and good education, and not only was fond of music, but had a very sweet voice. She loved to teaze our friend by singing to him a well-known ballad of that time, beginning

'Mich heute noch von dir zu trennen' &c.
(To have to part from thee to-day.)

"The favoured rival was the chief of the Austrian recruiting staff in Cologne, Carl Greth, whom Jeanette d'Honrath afterwards married.

"After this, a tender affection sprang up in his heart for a pretty, gentle girl, Fräulein von W——. I heard many anecdotes about his passion for this young lady from Bernhard Romberg (the celebrated violoncellist)."

These passing love episodes took place while he was growing into manhood, and left as little bitterness behind them, as they had awakened tender feeling in the fair one's breast.

"In Vienna, at all events, so long as I was there, from 1794-96, Beethoven was always in love with some one, and very often succeeded in making a conquest where many an Adonis would have found it most difficult to gain a hearing. I will also call attention to the fact that, as far as I know, each of Beethoven's beloved ones was of high rank."

This latter statement is confirmed in the larger biography, where, as in Leporello's song, countesses, baronesses, and ladies devoted to art, &c., all figure in turn, in rapid succession, though surely they must have allowed his devotion merely to teaze Beethoven, instead of truly loving him! There is still in existence a picture, in which Cupid is represented scorching Psyche's wing with a torch, and underneath is written in Beethoven's own hand:—

"A new year's gift for the tantalising Countess Charlotte Brunswick.
"From her friend,
"BEETHOVEN."

Among the many known women loved by Beethoven, we will mention the beautiful and gifted singer Magdalena Willmann, whom the great musician had befriended in his youthful days in Bonn. When he saw her again in Vienna, at the height of her power and beauty, he was so charmed with her, that he begged her to be his wife. But she refused, and why? "Because he was very ugly, and half crazy!" affirms one of Beethoven's biographers, who had it from one of the lady's nieces.

We must also mention one of his pupils, the young Countess Giulietta Giucciardi, who had a lovely figure, warm liquid blue eyes, and was only seventeen." "J'étais bien aimé d'elle et plus que jamais son époux," wrote her deaf master twenty years afterwards, in answer to a question on the subject addressed to him by his *Famulus*, to which we will add a note written by him to Wegeler, which confirmed the latter's knowledge of the great musician's love story. It reads :—

" Life has been a little brighter to me lately, owing to my mixing more with my fellows. I think you can have no idea how sad, how intensely desolate my life has been during the last two years. My deafness, like a spectre, appears before me everywhere, so that I flee from society, and am obliged to act the part of a misanthrope, though you know I am not one by nature.

"This change has been wrought by a dear fascinating girl, whom I love, and who loves me. After two years, I bask again in the sunshine of happiness, and now, for the *first time, I feel what a truly happy state marriage might be.* Unfortunately, she is not of my rank in life. Were it otherwise, I could not marry now, of course, so I must drag along valiantly. But for my deafness, I should long ago have compassed half the world with my art—I must do it still. There exists for me no greater happiness than working at, and exhibiting my art."

This was in the year 1801. Two years later the young countess married a Count Gallenberg, a composer of music for the ballet. Beethoven wrote with his own hand of her: "Et elle cherche moi pleurant, mais je la méprisais."

By this time he had attained a position which would have enabled him to marry, and it may be that he either proposed to the lady, or made his intentions so evident that there was no mistaking his purpose. But her courage was not greater than that of other ladies. Still, she must have felt her fault as deeply as a great sorrow, or she would not have 'sought him weeping'—she, a noble-born maiden of scarcely twenty years. Besides, is there not a kind of excuse for her conduct, half expressed in the exclamation Beethoven made when he characterised the step he had been inclined to take? *Famulus*, in speaking, or rather writing on the subject called it "The choice of Hercules," and Beethoven put an end to the subject by exclaiming: "And if I had given up inborn inspirations for marriage, what would have become of my higher, better self?"

We shall soon learn from the diary itself, that Beethoven seriously thought of devoting himself, to the exclusion of any closer tie, to his beloved art, and no doubt this was the final reason for his remaining unmarried to the end of his days.

His young pupil, Ries, who during the years 1801–5 lived on intimate terms with him, relates his impressions of the great musician on this subject as follows:—

"Beethoven had a great liking for female society, especially young and beautiful girls, and often when we met out of doors a charming face, he would turn round, put up his glass, and gaze eagerly at her, and then smile or nod, if he found I was observing him. He was always falling in love with some one, but generally his passion did not last long. Once when I teazed him on his conquest of a very beautiful woman, he confessed that she had enchained him longest, and most seriously of all, namely, *seven whole months*."

All of which is very good and pleasant, especially for an artist with his artist's taste for sensuous things, the highest of which being woman, can not only be understood but forgiven. But had not one of these power to move the innermost soul of the man, till his whole nature shook with the force of true passionate love?

The following account will answer for itself:—

In the secret drawer of an old cabinet, amongst a number of others, the marvellous letter, containing two postscripts, was found after his death, which first made known to the world the depth of the affectionate side of his nature, which his Sonatas had already more than revealed by their rich beauty and tender pathos.

The full, overflowing intensity of their expression we will not withhold, for may they not be the dark, but faithful background to the "unhappy love" he confessed to himself! To whom they were written no one knows. Some suppose it was to the young Countess Giulietta Giucciardi, but I think they err. Still less is it known for certain when this love was in progress—though it was most probably in the year 1806. The letters were written in pencil on the finest letter-paper, and evidently from some unknown watering-place, most likely in Hungary. Were they ever really sent? It is open to question. How, otherwise, did they come to be amongst Beethoven's papers? This one is dated the morning of July 6th:—

"My angel, my life, my self!—Only a few words to-day, written in pencil too—but with yours. My dwelling will be finally arranged to-morrow. What an immense amount of time is wasted over such things! Why this deep sorrow for things that cannot be altered? Would our love endure except through sacrifices and longings? Can you alter the fact that you are not mine, that I am not yours? Look around you at Nature and her lovely works, and let your sorrow be softened and consoled by the inevitable. Love demands everything, and rightly too; it is so with you; it is always so with me. If we were fully one, you would feel this pain as little as I should. We shall see each other soon. I cannot repeat to you to-day the remark I lately made about my life. If our hearts were always close together, such remarks would never be made. My heart is too full of you to tell you what it feels. Ah! there are moments in life when speech seems but a poor mode of expression. Cheer up, and be my true, loving, devoted one, as I am thine. All the rest we must leave in the hands of fate, that is, what is to be, and what must be. Thy true

"Ludwig."

But we have a still deeper glance into the man's passionate nature on the evening of the same day, when, lifted out of himself, and carried away with the intensity of his feeling, he writes:—

"You are in sorrow, my beloved—you suffer! Where I am, there thou art with me in spirit— With me and thee together! What a life!!! thus!—without thee. Kindness follows me everywhere; but they who merit kindness, often as little deserve it as they who offer it. Humility of man towards man pains me, when I contemplate my connection with the universe. What am I, and what is it, which could be called great? and yet herein lies the divine in man.

"I could weep when I think that you will not hear from me, probably, before Saturday. Much as you love me, I love you more, so never hide anything from me. Good night, I must go to sleep as I am taking the baths. Oh God, to be so near, and yet so far apart! But is not our love a true gift from heaven? It is as high and as durable as the blue vault above us!"

And as if sleep itself had not been able to interrupt the flow of his inward happiness, he continues the next morning:—

"*Good morning! July 7th.*—Even while I was still in bed, my thoughts flew over to you, my precious beloved one, sometimes happy ones, now and again of a nature to make me miserable, wondering what fate has in store for us. Live without you, I cannot, neither can I have you to myself; but I have determined to wander far away, till I can fly into your arms, till I can be wholly with you, my spirit will watch over you.

LOVE EPISODES. 109

Yes, it must be so : you will agree to this, for you know that I am faithful and true to you alone. No other could win my heart from you, no, never! Oh, it is hard, very hard, to go away from one so dear as you; why must it be so? My existence in Vienna is as painful as ever now. Your love renders me at once the most happy and the most miserable man alive. My age [he was five-and-thirty in 1806] requires a certain amount of uniformity in life; can this remain so in our present relations?

"My angel, I have just heard that the post goes every day. I must close this that you may have my letter sooner. You must be quiet and tranquil, for only by quiet waiting can we attain our end. Therefore, be patient—love me—to-day—yesterday—my heart and soul long for you with tears—for you—you my life (the writing becomes more hurried with each word) my all—farewell—love me more and more. Never doubt the faithful heart of thy lover.

'Always thine
Ever mine.
Each for the other to eternity.'
"L."

We will not follow too closely the reason for this hope in his life failing also, but pass on to remark that this summer of the year 1806, the Sonata in F flat (Op. 57) was finished, one of the most passionate outbursts of inward emotion from the hand of the great master, showing, as does the Apassionata, that it was written with the very heart-blood of the composer.

Stephan von Breuning, who had once been a rival of Beethoven's in an early love affair, in writing to an acquaintance at Bonn, in the fall of this same year, remarks that "Beethoven's frame of mind is generally of a melancholy turn."

We are tempted to place here an extract from Fraülein Giannatasio's pen, which also notices something more of this friend of his youth, Stephan von Breuning :—

"This refers,"—writes the young lady, speaking of an interesting conversation she had had with Beethoven on love and marriage, of which more anon—" This refers to what he once told us about a friend of his who also loved a girl he himself was in love with. The girl encouraged Beethoven. Was it from generosity, magnanimity, or what, that Beethoven left the field open to his friend and retired. The girl did not live very long. I believe she died soon after marrying Beethoven's friend."

Stephan von Breuning married, in 1808, the daughter of Beethoven's esteemed friend Dr. von Vering of Vienna. The young wife died eleven months after her marriage, just after Beethoven had dedicated to her the pianoforte part of a concerto work.

Again he was called upon to suffer with the passionate feelings of the musician and poet. The following extract from a letter to another friend, a Baron Gleichenstein of Freiburg, in the Breisgau, refers to this. He says:—

"Greet kindly for me all those who are dear to you and me. How willingly would I add, and to them to whom we are dear??? To me at least these notes of interrogation apply. Farewell and be happy, for I am not."

Baron Gleichenstein married, in 1811, Fräulein von Malfatti, whose beautiful and gifted sister, Therese, with dark auburn curling hair, and who was so volatile that she never regarded life seriously, yet made so deep an impression on Beethoven that he begged for her hand in marriage. A letter to his friend will tell us all we need to know about it. It runs:—

"Your news brought me down from the highest ecstasy to mundane regions. You wonder why I want any addition to my music. Am I then fit for nothing but music? So it seems, at least. I must henceforth lean on my own inner self, for, from the outward senses, I can obtain nothing. No, friendship and her sister feeling have given me nothing but wounds. So be it then! For thee, poor Beethoven, there is no outward happiness; only in the ideal world wilt thou find friends—everything must emanate from thy inward self."

"His marriage project is put an end to," wrote Stephan Breuning to his friend Wegeler, in August, 1810.

LOVE EPISODES.

Next we have Bettina, "the child." This charming and delightful friend of Goethe's inspired the great musician with a genuine artist's affection and devotion, during the spring of 1810, when she visited Vienna. She was worthy of admiration and devotion, even from a man of Beethoven's genius, for she had an intense appreciation of art, and was highly endowed with artistic talents herself. Even if we had no other proof of this, Beethoven's letter to her would be sufficient to demonstrate the well known fact. When she married the poet Achim von Arnim, Beethoven wrote to her :—

"May every happiness that can make marriage perfect be yours and your husband's. What shall I tell you of myself? 'Pity my fate,' I cry with Johanna. If I only live a few years longer, I will compass them as with weal and woe, and do much in them with the help of the Highest."

This was during the winter of 1811. In Beethoven's copy of the Odyssey, the following lines are marked :—

"For nothing is better or more desirable on earth
Than when man and wife, united in hearty love,
Calmly rule their house; a bitter sight to their enemies,
But a joy to their friends; and, to themselves, the highest enjoyment of all."

Then farther on, on one of the leaves of an album belonging to Fräulein Amalie Sebald, a couplet is written:—

"Ludwig van Beethoven,
Who, even if you wished,
Could not forget you."

Teplitz, August 8th, 1812.

About this time Beethoven was staying at the baths in Bohemia, where Fräulein Sebald, from Berlin, was also staying with a Russian family. She was a naturally gifted and well educated woman, of distinguished appearance, and about thirty years of age. Being endowed also with a sweet voice and great musical talent she naturally became attractive to Beethoven. We are in possession of a mass of short notes addressed to this lady by Beethoven, dating from almost the first day of their acquaintance. The feeling he had for her was not so much the warm, effervescent passion of youth, as the deep, quieter sentiment of personal esteem and affection, which comes later on in life, and, in consequence, is much more lasting.

"I a tyrant? You are, if you will!" he writes, September 12, 1812. "You cannot misunderstand what is said, unless your opinion is not in harmony with mine. No blame to you, therefore; on the contrary, it would more likely be to your happiness. The people say nothing, they are only people judging others by, and seeing others in, themselves; and that amounts to nothing. Away with it all! The good and the beautiful speaks each for itself. It requires no aid from any one, hence the foundation of our friendship.

"Farewell, dear Amelia. If the moon shines this evening brighter to me than the daylight, it will show you the least of all men by himself.

"Your friend,
"BEETHOVEN."

"The wave of genius ebbs by degrees," sings

Faust. It was the same with the emotions of this musician's master mind. We will give one more specimen of his feelings towards this lady :—

"What are you dreaming about, by saying you can be nothing to me? We will talk this over by word of mouth. I am ever wishing that my presence may bring peace and rest to you, and that you could have confidence in me. I shall hope to be better to-morrow, and that we shall be able to pass a few hours together in the enjoyment of nature while you remain here.

"Good-night, dear Amelia; many, many thanks for the proof you give me of your attachment to your friend,

"BEETHOVEN."

Another side to the contents of this letter, is the tender care given to the oft-suffering musician. He could not help feeling great affection and friendship towards one who was so good to him, and year by year he must have felt increasingly the want engendered by its absence. The year 1813 was one of suffering to him: "His life was a great misery from physical causes." A married lady friend of his, whom we shall hear more about later on, helped to restore him from the wretched state of despondency into which he had fallen, and from which he himself thought he should never recover, for the simple reason that his existence was wanting in all those tender surroundings which are almost indispensable for human happiness. His diary contains, under the date of the 13th of May, 1813, an appeal to himself and a cry for help from on High, which will explain for itself the terribly lonely state of the musician from whom every joy of the outside world seemed to pass, and leave him more lonely still It reads: "A great work to be accomplished, and yet to have to leave it unfinished. What, distinction is there in a useless, idle life, which has so often figured itself to me, and this—— What a fearful state to be in not to be able to trample under foot all my longings for home joys, to be constantly indulging in those longings.

O God! O God! look down in mercy upon poor, unhappy Beethoven, and put an end to this soon; let it not last much longer!"

With the year 1814, the Vienna Congress came to an end. Presents from the high and mighty, and especially from the generous Empress of Russia, after the great concert, helped considerably to place Beethoven in a more comfortable position as regards monetary matters. However, an invalid brother needed a large portion of these same gains, and then died, leaving his only son as a legacy to the generous brother who had so well befriended him in his last illness. This boy had to be cared for and educated, and Beethoven comforted himself when he undertook the duty by the knowledge that he had "rescued an innocent child from the hands of an unworthy mother." Soon after he bemoaned his misfortune to his pupil, Ries, then in London, in having placed the little lad at such a bad school that he felt obliged to start housekeeping, and have the boy to live with him at home.

This determination of his enables one to fully understand the closing expression in the letter addressed to Ries, March 8th, 1816. "Say everything that is kind to your wife. Unfortunately, I have none; I found only one, but I could not have her, still I do not on that account hate women."

In the summer of this year, 1816, he wrote:—

"Love, and love alone can give me a happy life. Oh God, let me find her who will keep me in the path of virtue, the one whom I may *rightly* call mine."

"*Baden, July 29th.*—When M—— was driving past it seemed to me that she looked at me."

Who could this M—— have been? We are not at all sure. The beautiful Therese Malfatti was not married to Baron von Drotzdick till the following year, 1817, and was living at that time in Vienna. Amalie Sebald had already espoused the Justizrath Krause.[*] Beyond this we can go no farther. But we have seen enough to judge for ourselves how, with the continual

[*] Councillor of Justice.

reawakening of his heart towards some attractive woman, inclination and necessity went hand-in-hand with the inward longing of his whole nature. Nay, more, because the very anchor of hope on which he leant for his future happiness, urged him, elderly and suffering as he was, to enter the state of matrimony, and yet, how was it that he failed to divine the tender womanly devotion which followed him so closely, while he was seeking for happiness afar? We shall refer to this again at the close of this chapter.

The young lady herself says:—

"He is cold and reserved with me, and I hide my grief down in the depths of my heart. Still, a short time since, my wish that we could make his life happier to him, seemed partially fulfilled. My people were kind to him, and he appeared thoroughly to understand our feelings of friendship for him, so that I was greatly rejoiced. Absent and occupied as I was with the heavenly beauty around us (the Helena Valley near Baden), I did not forget my duty. He spoke a great deal of the misery his loss of hearing causes him, and of the amount of physical suffering he goes through which obliges him to retire from society. This occupied us till we reached the Krämer huts."

Three weeks later on, 7th October, the young lady continues the account of his walk.

"It was very pleasant for me on our return home to reassure him on many points concerning the approaching operation on Karl, which I have no doubt had tormented him and made him anxious. I comforted him on the score of the nursing business, &c. At dinner in the valley he was in bright spirits; his muse inspired him too, and, as he wrote several bars, how I enjoyed it! He said to me, 'My walk with you has been fruitful in ideas; they will be reproduced later.'

"At Nanni's suggestion, I wrote and thanked Beethoven for the intense pleasure the day with him had given us, and then I felt comforted, for I had not been able to do it by word of mouth. How sad I felt, and how hard I found it to keep my heart still, as we went to breakfast with him, words fail me to express; yet it is inexpressibly sweet to me to render him a service by nursing his little Karl for him: he says he shall never be able to repay us. For myself this comforts me greatly, and I am glad he understands us."

She next refers to the operation, and writes:—

"*September* 28*th*.—I am now only able to write a few words on the operation which took place, and of our sympathy for the poor little sufferer. He will be dearer to us than ever now: one can't help being astonished at his great forwardness for his age. An inexpressible feeling of intense joy comes over me, each time I think that now we are in a position to render little Karl's good, noble uncle a service that he will always henceforth remember with gratitude.

"He was here to-day, and I spoke with him about Karl's mother, of his plans for the boy's future, &c. He looks forward to everything going well, and expressed a wish *to live with us*. Certainly that would be the best plan for him to adopt, but it cannot be carried out, on account of the summer-house. I never felt so certain, so convinced as I do now, that I should never have satisfied the cravings of his mind and his heart! Oh! he is so warm, so genuine, I feel sometimes as if I could and must be all in all to him. The longing desire to make his life brighter and happier for him makes me indulge in these foolish thoughts, but, as I say, I never before realised how unlikely this is."

We will insert here Beethoven's letter addressed to Father Giannatasio, Sept. 22nd, 1816.

"It is difficult sometimes to express the feeling, which will make you understand perhaps how inadequate words are, to convey to you my thanks for your news about Karl's operation. You must excuse my not being able to utter words which nevertheless I would fain have said.

"That I should wish to hear about the further progress of my dear little son, you will well understand. Since you were here, I have written to Bernard asking him to inquire of you for me, but I have received no reply to my letter as yet, and as he has evidently not been near you, you must take me for a heartless savage.

"It is impossible for me to be anxious about the boy when I know that he is nursed and tended by your excellent wife, but I would like to hear often about him; and that it pains me not to be able to assist in the alleviation of his sufferings, you will of course well understand; and, as it appears that I have trusted in vain in such a heartless unsympathising friend as Herr Bernard, you must not wonder if I appeal to your kindness, and beg for a line now and again to inform me of the child's welfare. With a thousand warm thanks to your noble, kind-hearted wife.

"In haste, yours,
"L. VAN BEETHOVEN."

Thus it appears that he was so deeply engaged on the " other things he had to think about " that he found it impossible to be present when his dearly loved son was operated on for hernia.

He was working then on one of his highest and noblest compositions, his Ninth Symphony which, at first, expressive of the deepest sorrow of human existence, finally rises into a jubilant cry of all-engrossing affection, in the "Freudeschönem Götterfunken."

A few days later he found time to pay a visit to the town, and seemed, as the young lady writes in her diary, in very good spirits, which no doubt was as much owing to the inward satisfaction he felt at the accomplishment of his great work, as at the joy he experienced in the care and tenderness surrounding his "beloved son." For the "activity," as he modestly termed his wonderful creative powers, seemed to have aroused the man's whole nature, and for the time being at least restored him to comparatively good physical strength and a healthy tone of mind.

The young lady writes:—

"*September* 29*th*.—Yesterday evening the 'dear uncle Beethoven' came to us again, bringing with him a young countryman of his. When

I told him that I believed he had returned to Baden, he laughed, and replied that he had given up believing. He was in *very good spirits*, of which I was truly glad. The song which I had lent him, he said he should bring me back at once, if only on account of my love of truth. The song is by Wessenberg, and called 'Mystery, Love, and Truth;' he was full of fun, and constantly made puns on different words."

In the fulness of his gratitude, he quite forgot that he had already written a warm, grateful letter expressive of his feelings, and a day or two following the evening above referred to, he wrote: "I forgot to say, I was in such a hurry, that all the love, tenderness, and care which Frau Giannatasio has bestowed on my little Karl during his illness, will ever be remembered by me with deep feelings of gratitude, and be inscribed in my debt-book as a debt I can never repay."

About this time the family at the head of the Institute were reduced through various unfortunate causes to a state of comparative penury, which made Beethoven, in several of his letters, promise to pay them double the amount agreed upon, for all the care and kindness they had bestowed on his beloved Karl. Whether he did so or not, the young lady does not mention. But we shall soon see that Beethoven himself was not long after this so reduced in his income, that he was obliged to give up his cherished plan of removing Karl from the Institute.

The song to which Fräulein Fanny refers, gives us a peep into the world in which Beethoven loved to dwell. It had been begun the year previous, but in the spring of 1816 it appeared in the supplement to the Vienna journal on 'Art, Literature, the Drama, and Fashion,' the editor of which was Beethoven's "unsympathising friend" Bernard. Beethoven's borrowing it can be accounted for in a very practical way; the young "countryman" to whom we have referred being no other than a son of the great music publisher, Simrock, from Bonn, who published it in the following year.

The text is as follows, translated into English.

THE SECRET.

Where blooms the flower which doth not fade?
Where is the star which e'er doth shine?
Tell me, O Muse, in what fair glade
To seek that flower and star divine.

I cannot teach thee where to find
These treasures, if thou canst not tell.
The star and flower are in the mind;
Thrice happy they who guard them well!

And the music to this tender, simple song, on the charm of love and truth, intended rather to be recited than sung, came straight from the heart of the singer, touching with a sympathising chord the hearts of those who heard it. This is shown by the superscription: "To be played with great feeling, but not dragged," which words Beethoven dotted down in the little note-book which was full of sketches of his Sonata, op. 106, and the Ninth Symphony. To this little circumstance we owe the date of the time when the greatest work of Beethoven's genius was begun—thus proving how often small incidents tend to determine with certainty the time when the deepest feelings in an artist's soul were stirred, and the grand creations of his brain were first revolving in his mind. We shall soon, however, find that, while absorbed in the ideal life natural to the creation of such a great work, and separated so to speak from daily life, he was in the greatest perplexity, and fighting constant battles with real existence. The trivialities and unavoidable wants of each day were necessary to his physical state, even when the flights of inspiration put him on a pinnacle beyond the reach of ordinary men. About this time he was attacked by a malady of the lungs, which did not leave him till the following summer. Truly may it be said, that artists have plenty of sorrow in their struggle through life!

The young lady goes on:—

"*November 1st.*—The suffering state of our beloved Beethoven is a matter of great concern to me. Ill, and surrounded by unsympathising people, without any near ties or joys. He! It is fearful to think of! Yesterday it delighted me to hear from father that he had expressed again a wish to come and live with us, and the consciousness that he begins to regard us as true friends, sweetens to me the bitterness of the thought that he has no friend, that he is, as he himself says, 'alone in the world!' What would I not give if this noble, unique man could have a life of genuine true happiness."

Beethoven himself enlightens us on this subject in a letter addressed about this time to Father Giannatasio, in which he says:—

"My household resembles very much a shipwreck; if not quite, it is at least approaching that state. My health also does not seem in too great a hurry about restoring itself to its old condition." Under such circumstances it was evidently not possible for him to engage a tutor for the boy and have him at home with him in his own house; therefore, he begged Father Giannatasio to allow the child to remain at the Institute for another quarter, adding also that he must talk the matter over, and discuss certain points of the boy's education, which "unfortunately these hard times oblige me to do." This was the year of the famine, 1816–17. We shall presently see how this affected Beethoven.

The young lady goes on:—

"*November* 10*th.*—While Nanni, Leopold, and papa were gone to see the entry of the new Empress (Caroline of Bavaria) I intended taking advantage of the quiet hour to write a long letter to Duncker. But when I set about it, I found it so difficult to put my thoughts into words that I gave it up in despair, and merely penned him a few lines telling him of the joy it was to me to see Beethoven again, adding to my expression of how kind he was to me, the hope that he will live amongst us many years yet, although he is evidently anxious about his health. I am childish enough to feel wounded because he seems to prefer Nanni to me, although I have told myself a thousand times that I have no right or pretensions to his showing a preference for me. I do not quite like his calling me the 'Lady Abbess' when I am busy with my housekeeping; for the thoughts I know he associates with this title, I would rather he did not have about me. It does not please me at all for him to regard me simply in the light of a good housekeeper, any more than that Leopold should look upon Nanni, as a lady only fit for company. Now, if I could watch over and care for him, I would do it with pleasure! Does he not deserve to have some loving, thoughtful being about him always? Now and then I have pictured to myself my taking this care of him *without*, however, any *closer* tie binding us together. It surely would please him, if he only knew it, that it would be intense happiness to me if I might make his life pleasurable to him by simply attending to household duties for him."

We will insert here a little note of Beethoven's which proves that he appreciated the care taken of himself and his adopted son, and that he regarded the young lady as his helper, or rather adviser, in other things, besides the material comforts necessary for Karl. He writes:—

"The high and well-born Frau A. Giannatasio is kindly entreated to inform the undersigned, who finds it difficult to keep the number of trousers, socks, shoes, &c., in his head, how many yards of cashmere are required for his active young nephew, and to reply at once without further reference to your humble servant.

The lady abbess will be consulted this evening on affairs relating to Karl, if he remains.

"L. v. BEETHOVEN."

About this time, the poor hard-working musician was assailed by troubles and worries of another kind. The "queen of night" spared no pains in wreaking her revenge on him, and Karl began to grow indolent and idle. Writing to Giannatasio, he says :—

"I should like very much to know what effect my treatment of Karl has had on him, since you last complained of him. Since then I have been delighted to find him very impressionable to a sense of honour. We were very quiet to each other, he timidly pressed my hand, but I did not return the caress. He ate scarcely any dinner, and said he felt very unhappy, though he would not then tell me why. At last, while we were out walking, he confessed that he was unhappy because he had not been so industrious lately as he used to be formerly. I thereupon gave him a little of my mind on the subject, and warmed in my manner towards him. He is evidently tender in feeling, which trait in his character makes me hope great things for him."

The poor man was undeceived soon enough. Fräulein Fanny's impression that a well ordered household with a wife and mother at its head would be the best help for him here, is certainly right. But his love of peace and quiet, "two great blessings," and a certain amount of shyness in undertaking such "ties," seemed to prevent his thinking much about them, while the bitterness of delay, necessitated by his constant daily duties, grew stronger and stronger.

He writes to Giannatasio:—

" As regards the mother, she has openly expressed a wish to see Karl with me. You must have often observed how I hesitated before placing any confidence in her. I dislike imputing motives to actions, all the more so now that she cannot do Karl any harm. I think you can well understand how a man like myself, accustomed to frank, open dealings with all my fellows, shrinks from these sort of things into which, for Karl's sake, I am unwillingly drawn, especially all that concerns his mother. I should be glad never to hear another word on the subject."

The young lady continues:—

"*November* 17*th*, 10·30 P.M.—Beethoven was here to-day, and looking so well and strong, that I do not feel anxious about the bad effects of his late illness. While the others lingered at table, I had a pretty long conversation with him: it is some time now since I have enjoyed chatting to him so much. Everything he says, every one of his sentiments are worthy of record. Foolish and silly as it seems to write it, yet I can't help myself, when I say that it really pains and hurts me to see his preference for Nanni to me. He had been talking to me for about half an hour when she came in, and immediately he brightened up, and seemed to *forget* my presence.

"What more do I want, silly girl that I am? I ought to be satisfied that he cares for me as much as he does. I have no right to expect more; besides, I ought to be ashamed of myself for giving way to this affection for him so soon after my late bitter sorrow, when I know that it brings me many hours of misery. My intuitions are generally correct, and I find it difficult to cast them out of my thoughts, but I fear me greatly I shall have to *live my life without* the love I long for. What I feel is the need of loving and being loved, the right of being sympathised with, my *soul infused in another soul*. That this wish should arise from knowing a man like Beethoven, seems a natural thing to me, and *because* the wish is there, I do not think I am so unworthy of him; in time, the very force of my feelings for him must be felt by him."

"*November 23rd.*—Yesterday we went to the first representation of Abbé Stadler's Oratorio

'The Deliverance of Jerusalem.' I cannot refrain from repeating what I have written before, that I have no taste or inclination for dress, society and amusement, although I dare say I carry this out too far. Still I *feel* I am *no longer* young. Perhaps the chief reason for this dislike of mine to society arises from the fact that my time is, as a rule, entirely taken up in domestic duties which are apt to make one look upon other things as frivolous. If I could dress to please *one* alone, that would be a very different affair. But, alas! this one does not exist for me. I know one whom I would like to so please, but he never gives me a thought, at least not in this special way.

"The music was very good, but to Nanni's and my taste, it lacked 'earnest sweetness.' But this one unique man, our beloved friend, is to blame for this, he has taught us to look for it everywhere."

"*December 5th.*—A day or two ago, Beethoven came to see us in the morning, and we had such an interesting conversation, or rather he told us so much that interested us about himself, that I was quite pleased, and yet he told us other things that quite upset me. We shall most probably lose him soon. He means to leave the town where his great worth is only partially recognised. How sad things are here! He was right when he exclaimed that art had to work for butchers and bakers. If it is for his good, then, I must learn to bear the pain his absence will cause me, and give up the hope I have indulged in sometimes of making life easier for him, by superintending his household cares for him. I wonder if we shall ever see him again, or hear from time to time how he is! Whether or no, God's will be done; in our hearts he will always be with us, as I hope he will not forget us. This is my only comfort."

The young lady refers to the long contemplated journey to London. On the 18th of December, 1816, a few days after the above-mentioned conversation, Beethoven wrote to the young composer, Ch. Neate, then in London, that he should feel "flattered" to write a Symphony or Oratorio for the Philharmonic Society. He presumed (and rightly) that in England he was more highly esteemed as a composer than at home, and that in character and disposition he felt he had a great affinity with the "haughty Englishmen"—as they were called at that time. The journey was neither then, nor at any subsequent period, undertaken, and yet the completion of his great work, the Ninth Symphony was due to a commission from this same English Philharmonic Society!

We will let the young lady continue.

"*December 16th.*—Yesterday I passed a very pleasant day in Beethoven's society. He was in good spirits, and, if I mistake not, was more than usually kindly disposed towards us. With the greatest patience and good nature, he answered all our numerous questions and inquiries about himself, adding so many other interesting details on various subjects, that I felt as if I should never weary of listening to him. And as I always imagine that he thoroughly knows many things besides what simply concern his art, I was especially delighted to have my convictions thus openly confirmed."

"*December* 20*th*.—Another still more delightful evening with Beethoven. To Nanni's intense pleasure he dedicated to her the new song he has just composed, the manuscript of which she will preserve as a relic."

This song was the 'Ruf vom Berge' (song from the hills) composed on the 13th of December, just a few days previously, and is a delightful specimen of that exquisite simplicity, which is the characteristic charm of Beethoven's ballad compositions. Here at least there is no hint of sorrow or old age, the creative genius of the musician is eternally young. The author of the words is a Friedrich Treitschke, who in the year 1841 inspired Beethoven to write the air for Floristan in 'Fidelio' by his lines :—

"Und spür ich nicht linde, sanft säuselnde Luft,
Und ist nicht mein Grab mir erhellet?" &c.

SONG FROM THE HILLS.

If but a bird were I,
And I had wings: to thee,
Dear love, I'd fly.
But no, that cannot be;
In vain I sigh!

If but a star were I,
And twinkled in the night
High in the sky,
Thou would'st gaze at my light
And wish me nigh!

If but a brook were I
That rippled 'neath the sun,
I'd ne'er be shy;
I'd kiss thy feet, when none
Were passing by!

Were I the evening breeze
In spring, I'd breathe on thee
From balmy west;
Thy bosom and thy lips to me
Would be sweet rest!

The livelong night I wake
To think of thy dear face,
And oft I take,
In thought, one loving gaze!
My heart doth break!

The brook, the star, the wind,
And birds all haste away
My love to find,
But I alone must stay,
Banished! behind!"

The young lady goes on :—

"On *December* 26*th*, St. Stephen's Day, we were quite alone in the evening, and I was just beginning to lose all hope that he would come in as he does sometimes on Sunday evening, when at last he appeared. This time it was not such a pleasure to me as usual. At first he only spoke in monosyllables, and sat reading the almanack most of the time he was with us. We agreed afterwards that he must have been suffering, besides being in an excessively bad humour, through the vexation he has received at the hands of the burghers! Father was in a rage with the public of last Wednesday, who not only could not appreciate the great master's works, but have no desire to place him on the pinnacle of fame."

By way of explanation, we must here give an extract from the report of the Vienna musical journal of this year's Concert for the benefit of the poorer inmates of the general hospital, which took place as usual on Christmas Day. "The concert opened with Beethoven's Symphony (the Seventh) in A sharp, very difficult of execution, but under the conduct of this gifted composer, performed with the greatest precision. That the applause was not very clamorous, and that the favourite Andante was not, as usual, encored, can only be accounted for by the fact that the dense crowding of the audience hindered the free use of their hands."

A somewhat remarkable excuse!

But Beethoven's disappointment must have been all the greater, because even in "his iron time" as he writes, and on account of the many expenses on his nephew's behalf, he had hoped to increase his income by giving a concert himself, and the feeble sympathy shown by the public to one of his noblest creations, gave him little hope of the success of his intended undertaking. This was a further inducement to carry out his plan of going to London.

The young lady continues:—

"But the evening ended much more pleasantly than it had begun. Beethoven teased us like a child at times. I have often marvelled over the genuine child-like nature he displays sometimes. We poked fun at one another, and it was owing to this brighter mood of his *before* he went, that I did not break down afterwards when I sang that wondrous song by him, 'To my absent beloved one.' How can I help my whole soul being filled with his image? Wherever I am, whatever I am doing, even to the smallest household duty, I *feel* his presence with me, filling me with the sweetest joy.

"Even when I am at the Rohmann's, where there is nothing to remind me of him, I still feel his spirit hovering near me, imbuing me with the tenderest sadness. But even this sadness was at times painful, under the influence of certain songs."

In order fully to understand the young lady's feelings, and still more to sympathise with one of the deep emotions of Beethoven's soul, we refer our readers to this song to an absent beloved one, of which the simple words express a spirit of tender yearning for the presence of the beloved being, and were written by a poet and scholar who was greatly admired at that time in Vienna. Beethoven regarded the words as an "impulse or a happy inspiration," which is well expressed in the music.

This song was composed in the year 1815-16, just before the sorrow overtook him, of his own "unhappy love affair" in Baden. Perhaps the great musician had some special lady in his mind, when he wrote the sweet music for this song—who can say? Is it necessary to know, in order to understand the music?

If these simple words are "sung instead of read," as Goethe wrote, when he sent his songs into the world, we shall be able to sympathise with the emotion of the young lady, with her poetical temperament, when, a few days later on, she saw the great master who first sang, and then rendered these lines immortal, by the power of his genius.

She writes :—

"*December* 29*th*.—I had scarcely laid my pen aside yesterday, when we were surprised by a visit from our delightful friend, Beethoven. I was all the more charmed with this proof of his friendship for us, as it was quite unexpected on our part, and evidently arose from a liking on his side to be with us. I am glad to notice that we are now on very intimate terms with him. He must enjoy our friendship, and appreciate it more than formerly."

Then comes the following candid confession:—

"*January* 11*th*, 1817.—This morning I heard from Leopold that M—— has formally demanded Lotte of her mother. Many mixed feelings are working within me at this moment, and making me weep involuntarily, notwithstanding the joy this news has given me. This evening, Beethoven will be here, as he has been almost every day now for the last week. I am inexpressibly happy that he seems to cling to us. Little incidents often arouse within me bitter, sad feelings that might truly be termed jealousy; as, for instance, his significant reply to Nanni's childish question, in reference to a ring he wears, as to whether he loves any one else besides his 'absent beloved one.' Still these feelings arise from the thought that no happy love is reserved for me, and that I ought not to be astonished at such a man as Beethoven showing preference for one, who is more likely to rouse his interest in her.

"*Morning.*—To-day my dear, happy Lotte comes! She once went through the same doubts and sorrows as I am doing now. May be mine will turn into joy, as hers have done! May this hope be blessed!"

"*January* 19*th.*—We have had an excessively interesting evening with Beethoven. He accompanied his 'Absent beloved one,' while Nanni sang it. I seemed to be absorbed while he was playing; my very soul was wrapped in the music, and a heavenly rapture overpowered me as I listened! At last, after all our patience, we were rewarded to the *full!* He was *so* good-natured to us, and our fear that the evening might be somewhat 'slow,' on account of the Schönauers, was quite groundless as matters turned out."

The young lady, referring again to such delicious moments, writes :—

"Once when he brought me the text of his 'Absent beloved one,' father expressed a wish for me to accompany my sister while she sang it. But Beethoven put a summary end to my anxiety by simply saying, 'Be off with you,' and seated himself at the piano. But I must add that several times he went wrong; and on my sister asking him if she had not made a mistake, or something to that effect, he replied, as he pointed to one place, where no connecting mark was traced, 'Very well, indeed,—but here,' alas! he had not heard her."

And the young lady goes on to add that Beethoven, while accompanying this song, "sat there quite rapt." She makes a slight mistake, however, in saying that the great master brought her this song for the first time on that special evening—since she had had it for some time.

The diary continues :—

"I ought to have checked my growing and all-absorbing interest in this noble being, but it is beyond me now. I cannot put aside or crush out of existence the intense joy the thought gave me that he would spend a few days with us during the summer. There is a world of hidden meaning in those few words. If he only would! Well, and what then? Ah, then I might have hoped! And now, now I dare not even *hope!*"

Here we will close this chapter on Beethoven's love episodes, and begin a fresh one through which the tender, earnest friendship of this young lady will shine steadily, helping us to develop further the character of the great musician. She, with her womanly heart, will worthily unfold to our knowledge the nature and manner of the gifted being whom accident threw across her path in life, and guide our steps to the right understanding of him through her own deep and genuine love of his beloved art.

CHAPTER V.

SORROW.

How very unfit Beethoven was for the task he proposed to himself in the education and management of his nephew, can be seen at a glance in the account we have given of his artist's career, added to which there was the continual and ever-increasing anxiety and trouble, caused by the "queen of night."

Often forced, from the difficulties which surrounded him, to seek help from his friends concerning his nephew, yet, when it was willingly granted him, he did not seem to value and appreciate it; and, again and again, wounded them by his disregard of their feelings, and the constant want of confidence he displayed towards them. It is not a pleasant task to record his shortcomings on this head; nevertheless, we are bound so to do, not only to prove the genuineness of the friendship itself, but to be in a position to judge fairly of the whole relations between him and this family.

We will first follow the diary.

"*January 27th.*—I am quite upset by the report of the little one who has just returned from his uncle, who is ill; he says that he is very sad."

"*January 31st.*—Yesterday morning Nanni had a long conversation with our dear Beethoven, in which she tells me they discussed art, and then talked about some letters and presents he had received from a Bremen maiden."

What the presents were we are not informed, but the "Bremen maiden" was a daughter of Dr. W. C. Müller, called Elise, an enthusiastic admirer of Beethoven. She played his compositions in public in her native town of Bremen.

About this time the friendly intercourse between Beethoven and the Giannatasio family was interrupted. The following entry speaks for itself.

"*March 1st.*—That Beethoven is vexed with us is a very great trial to me, but that he should show it in the way he does adds to its bitterness. It is true that father has not behaved very well to him; still, I think that Beethoven ought not to retort with biting sarcasm, when he knows how much affection and interest we have always had for him. I expect he wrote that letter in one of his misanthropical humours, and I forgive him truly for it. We have not seen him since the evening when Nanni and I were ill in bed."

The letter alluded to is certainly somewhat sharp and decided in its tone concerning Karl's instruction in music—for the lad had now begun studying music—but "biting sarcasm" could scarcely be discovered in it, unless by one who, like this young lady, felt for this great master the sensitive friendship natural under existing circumstances. We will quote the essential part of this letter that it may speak for itself, merely stating, by way of explanation, that the well-known Vienna composer, Czerny, had been a pupil of Beethoven, and was now Karl's music-master. He writes:—

"It was, at least, the first time that I had to be reminded of a pleasant duty, owing to pressing business, not only connected with my art, but with other things as well. I need hardly say it shall not happen again. I thank you very much for your kindness in sending your servant yesterday to fetch Karl; as I knew nothing about it, it might have happened that he would have had to remain at Czerny's."

It is as well to remark here, that the reason for Beethoven's laying such stress on the boy's being "fetched," arose from the fact that Karl's mother was in the habit of watching her son's comings and goings, partly to satisfy her mother's longing to try and see her child, and partly for the purpose of calumniating his uncle and guardian to the Courts of justice, or to lower him in the estimation of the public. The latter she succeeded in so effectually, that some time after, during the later law proceedings, she had the "sympathy of the public" entirely on her side.

As regards the mother's seeing her son at all, Beethoven writes that each attempt was followed by a bitter pang in the boy's heart, which did him more harm than good; and he adds, "the rumours concerning this bad woman have so upset me that I am fit for nothing to-day—on no account would I have Karl hear them." Another point of weighty importance with Beethoven was Karl's musical studies. He had pictured to himself his nephew's future career as that of a great musician, and one of the chief sources of rupture with the Institute arose out of deficient attention to the boy's practice on the piano.

The letter continues :—

"As regards his practice on the piano, I must beg you to be firm with him and keep him to it, otherwise his lessons are of no use. Yesterday he did not touch the piano, and I know this has happened many times, because I take upon myself to go over with him what he is doing, that I may judge how he progresses."

"'La musica merita d' esser studiata.' (Music requires study.)

"The couple of hours devoted to this art are scarcely sufficient; and I must entreat that he is strictly kept to them. It is not an uncommon thing, after all, for attention to be paid to this branch of art in an Institution like yours."

Beethoven's vexation was certainly very great; but, as we go on, we shall see that many misunderstandings arose between Beethoven and the Giannatasio family from a want of truth on Karl's part. The letter closes thus:

"With every expression of respect,
"Your friend,
"L. VAN BEETHOVEN."

The young lady continues:

"*March 6th.*—I am quite grieved at Beethoven's behaviour to all of us, though my vexation has gone. I long now for the stupid affair to be over and finished, and even if I do not often see him, to know and be sure that he thinks of us in his heart with feelings of kindness and affection. I am not sure that he does now; and both Nanni and I grieve over it night and day, it distresses us even in our dreams. It is really too bad! If he only knew how many unhappy hours he has caused us, and could see for himself how little *we two* deserve such treatment at his hands! Surely he must feel in his heart how we care for him—and will come to us and make it all up—and be friends again!"

The young lady did not write in her diary for a week following the above entry; then, on the 15th of March, we have:—

"I have just read over my last entry with strangely pleasant feelings—for he *has* been to us, and we *are friends again*. It has pained me very deeply to be obliged to acknowledge how much Karl has been to blame in all these misunderstandings, and it grieved me still more deeply that we were forced to inform his uncle of several misdemeanours of his, which have angered him beyond measure.

"When Nanni asked Beethoven if he was

still vexed with us, he answered, 'I do not estimate myself high enough for that.' He did not however thaw in his manner towards us until the little misunderstanding which had led to our dissension had been explained on both sides. Father's want of tact about fetching Karl, the botheration about the money for Karl's music lessons, and the boy's falsehood about his not being allowed to practice, all seemed to have an irritating effect upon his somewhat depressed state of mind, and made him involuntarily hesitate at placing the confidence in us we deserved. At least, so it appears to me. However, he came —and seemed slightly embarrassed—perhaps because he regrets having written that letter; however, I hope all will go well now, and I trust he will be for the future as friendly as formerly. I have never before been so satisfied with my expectations as I am now. If only my desire could be carried out, and he could be made to perceive that we mean kindly by him,—if this wish of mine were only truly understood, then we might be able to ameliorate some of his sad hours, and make his life a little brighter for him."

Any way, if Beethoven put aside his want of confidence in the family, he did not do the same with the Institute, for he rarely allowed himself to visit there now. The young lady remarks in her diary, under date the 2nd of May :—

"Our dear Beethoven we rarely see now. I pity him with all my heart, with that nephew of his, who I fear will cause him a great deal of sorrow. How willingly would I ease his brow of all this care if I could! His last song 'North or South' has given us so much pleasure."

The music of this song was composed and published in this same winter (1816-17), and gives us an insight into Beethoven's feelings at a time when, while struggling against continual, and ever-increasing troubles, he was arming himself with a growing consciousness of a higher glory to be gained for his art, which glory he meant to attain to his own satisfaction.

The words were written by Karl Lappe. We

quote a few of the lines as a sample of their bombastic style.

NORTH OR SOUTH.

North or South what's it to me?
If there the glorious heaven I see!
If there fair beauty and beloved art
Still find a place within the warm, glad heart.
The North cannot destroy the strong in soul and mind;
The feeble only die through winter's wind.
North or South, what do I care,
If but a glowing heart be ever with me there!

Mysterious death and sweet refreshing sleep;
Welcome, twin brothers, with your slumbers deep!
The day is o'er; you close the weary eyes,
And lovely scenes before the mind arise.
The day is brief, and life is far too short,
Why doth it try to charm, and yet remaineth not?
Mysterious sleep or death—why should I either fear?
When morning dawns, then all is bright and clear!

The next few pages of the diary are not of sufficient importance to quote here. In order to be near his nephew, Beethoven had changed his apartments in the spring to some nearer the Institute, fixing upon a house in the very same suburb, the Landstrasse.

The young lady writes:—

"*May* 13*th*.—Yesterday, Beethoven came to see us, after a tolerably long absence. He *breathes* in *our atmosphere*, and his creative brain is no doubt busy with compositions that a hundred years hence will still be wondered at for their marvellous beauty! And these works are being written in *our* neighbourhood! How I wish he could be free of every outside worry, while his creative powers are thus in progress. No wonder it often makes him feel upset and ill to come in contact with cold, ordinary, unsympathetic people who wound him without knowing it; he who ought never to be pained or disturbed with anything or by any one!"

To fully understand the above, we will quote a letter of Beethoven's, dated the 19th of June, 1817, addressed to his "Father Confessor," the Countess Erdödy: "Too much have I been upset lately, and I have had too many troubles, besides being ill off and on since the 6th of October, 1816! Day after day I hope to get rid of my suffering state, and although I am somewhat better lately, still I think I am taking a long while to get quite well again.

"You may imagine how this state of things distresses me! My deafness is growing worse; formerly it rendered it a very difficult matter for me to attend to my wants, how much more so now that I have my brother's child to provide for as well. My difficulties I try to alleviate by turning first to one and then to another, but everywhere I am left alone, and become the spoil, so to speak, of bad, designing people. A thousand times I have thought of you, my dear, kind friend, and I still think of you, but my *own misery weighs me down completely*."

Thoughts of approaching death became day by day more familiar to him, and about this same date he wrote on the little composition, 'The Monk's song,' from Schiller's 'Tell,' "In memory of the swift and unexpected death of our Krumpholz, May 3, 1817." Beethoven was acquainted with this violinist, who had suddenly dropped down dead in the street the day before. The lines of this song ran as follows:—

> "Rasch tritt der Tod den Menschen an,
>   Es ist ihm keine Frist gegeben.
> Es stürzt ihn mitten in der Bahn,
>   Es reisst ihn fort vom vollen Leben.
> Bereitet oder nicht, zu gehen,
>   Er muss vor seinem Richter stehen!"

> (Death swiftly seized upon his prey;
>   No respite to the man was given;
> He met him, in his own dread way,
>   And tore him from among the living.
> Prepared or not, he still was driven
> To meet his Judge—for hell or heaven!)

This year of 1817 was a very poor one in respect to compositions.

The next entry stands:—

"*June 1st.*—I rarely see Beethoven now. It grieves me terribly that he stays away from us so much. Still I am somewhat comforted by knowing that he does at bottom care for us!"

In reference to the following extract, dated the 15th of June, we must observe that the Herr Pacher therein mentioned was a young widower with two little daughters, who, at that time, was staying at Giannatasio's establishment. As his appearance and manners reminded Fräulein Fanny very vividly of her deceased lover, what would have been more natural than that an affection should have gradually sprung into existence for him in her heart, especially as she had long before arrived at the conclusion that the great musician, who was friendly with the whole family, would never be anything more than a friend to her? But she would not allow herself to encourage any such hopes. She writes:—

"I awoke this morning from a dream which for a while made me feel very wretched. I dreamed that we had all been greatly mistaken in Pacher's character, and that he whom I regarded as my worthy lover, and my relatives looked upon as a dear friend, had proved himself to be beneath the trust we reposed in him. This dream made me think of him, some time later on, in a new and interesting light, and I unconsciously confounded him with my dear deceased lover. In case, however, that, in the course of time, I should grow to value his sterling worth, and, as is just possible, my calm, indifferent feeling towards him may develop into something warmer, I will take the precaution of being on my guard, as we are to be in the same house together, and not only will not seek his society, but be very sincere with myself, busy myself with other things, and then wait and see if he takes any interest in me or not; for *him* whom I would rather please than any one else, I must be content to do without.

"To-day I was more than ever carried away by the wonderful power of his creative genius! His music always stirs me to the very innermost depths of my soul, and makes me feel an enthusiasm for him, which is increased, if possible, when I think of him as a man, moreover, who possesses many sterling qualities of character."

The young lady then goes on to give us many details about Beethoven, which explain, to a certain degree, the happiness and unhappiness of his life. She writes:—

"He and Nanni, lately had a short but very interesting chat on love and marriage. He is certainly a peculiar man in many things, and his ideas and opinions on this subject are still more peculiar. He declares that he does not like the idea of any indissoluble bond being *forced* between people in their personal relations to each other. I think I understand him to mean that man or woman's *liberty* of action ought not to be limited. He would much rather a woman gave him her love, and with her love the highest part of her nature, without, as he means, being bound to him in the relation of wife to husband. He believes that the liberty of the woman is limited and circumscribed.

"He spoke of a friend of his who was very happy, and who had several children, who, nevertheless, held to the opinion that marriage without love was the best for man. But we did not agree with his friend's ideas on marriage, any more than we did with his own. As far as his experience went, he said that he did not know a single married couple who, on one side or the other, did not repent the step he or she took in marrying; and that, for himself, he was excessively glad that not one of the girls had become his wife whom he had passionately loved in former days, and thought at the time it would be the highest joy on earth to possess; and then he added that it was often a good thing that man could not always have his wishes fulfilled.

"I will not repeat my answer, but I believe *I know* a *girl* who, beloved by him, would *not* have made his life unhappy. On the other hand, would she have made it happy?

"Nanni remarked that he would always be more devoted to his art than to any wife, if he had one. That, he replied, was quite natural, and that he could never love a wife who would not be able to honour his art. *Basta!*"

This Italian exclamation, "*Basta*, enough!" was quite sufficient, we agree, to put an end to the wishes of the young lady and make her renounce them for ever. Her communications, however, continue to be imbued with the same spirit of deep sympathy for the unhappy fate of the great musician.

The next entry is dated the 25th of June:—

"Yesterday, Beethoven was quite upset, and overcome with the sadness of the affair about Karl's mother. Our sympathy, and talking it over with us, seemed to do him good."

. We will quote a few words from Beethoven's own diary on this fresh vexation and trouble.

"O God! Thou seest me forsaken by all the world; but an injustice I will never do. Grant my supplication, that I may spend my future with my Karl, for as yet it does not seem very possible! O, hard fate, cruel destiny; no, no, my miserable state will never end!"

The young lady writes from memory:—

"A new state of life, if I may so call it, now began for Beethoven: he seemed determined to devote himself body and soul to the boy, and whether he had pleasure and joy in him, or was entangled in difficulties, or bowed down with grief, he could not or would not write it."

It was for the first time in his life that he

experienced the feeling of having a human being entirely dependent on him, whom he had voluntarily drawn to his side from an impulse that urged him to seek love and affection in some domestic tie, while believing, with the passion of his own nature, that the close relationship would be for his own and the boy's future good.

How true is the old saying that dropping water will wear away stone! Thousands of charming impressions which might hold their influence through life, fostered by the affection of parents, are often banished from memory under the stiff discipline of school life. "Karl is quite another boy when with me," writes Beethoven in his diary, in the spring of this same year, "which strengthens me in the plan of having him with me always. Besides, it will spare me many a heartache caused by that (Institute)."

The young lady writes:—

"*July 8th.*—I have written to Beethoven about a letter of his to Karl, but it has not reached him yet. I cannot endure the idea of a quarrel between us. He cannot misinterpret the contents of my letter, for it contains the truth, and expresses an esteem and admiration for him on our part, which cannot fail to be pleasant to him. The thought is certainly disagreeable to me, that there is truth in father's accusation, that Beethoven's conduct is at times very inconsistent. But how can he (Beethoven) believe that father could act to Karl as he says he does. If I were once to admit such an idea into my head, I should be most miserable."

Day by day Beethoven grew more and more suspicious about the way in which his nephew was treated, and began to make the life of those miserable, who were concerned in the lad's education. At last, matters came again to a climax.

The diary continues:—

"*July* 21*st*.—Taken as a whole, yesterday was a very pleasant day. But the day previous several things happened which tended not a little to interrupt the usual quiet tenor of my life. First, there was that letter to Beethoven, which reached him at last, in which I put before him, far more forcibly than was possible in conversation, his suspicions respecting Karl, and our sentiments on the matter."

She adds later on :—

"As regards Beethoven's opinion of us, I am very glad to be able to fall back upon my old idea, that he understands our feelings towards him. I cannot help it, if my peace of mind depends upon being sure that he does not misjudge us or our actions."

"*August* 10*th*.—Since then a number of small vexations have occurred with Beethoven, finally crowned with one worse than all that had gone before. But for Nanni's courageous and plucky mode of acting, we should have been overwhelmed with sorrow and vexation. I have a horror of meddling in other people's affairs. May be, however, if *I* had been the cause of this unfortunate disagreement, I should have yielded at once, in order that peace might be restored. Nanni and I could scarcely await with patience the arrival of Herr Pacher to confide in him, whom we look upon as a trustworthy friend, our fresh grief and trouble. It was all right again by the time he came, and I found it difficult to suppress the joy I felt. All the more so because he rejoiced with us, and seemed as delighted as we were. When Karl returned from Czerny's, he brought me a message from his uncle, begging me not to show my father the letter that had been *written* in a *rage* and *in such blind fury*. Thus all was well.

"As I was returning home yesterday, I was overjoyed at seeing Pacher pass by. Joyous, but somewhat dissatisfied with myself, I turned back in the rain, and, on reaching home, I saw Beethoven's letter to father, in which he writes in such an injured tone about me, that I felt not only pained, but excessively angry. I could not bear it; so I took a pen and wrote down immediately my sentiments on the matter. Never before have I had such a bitter experience, and the fact that it is caused by one whom I reverence so highly, makes it all the more bitter to bear. If Duncker only knew that Beethoven should think I could be so *mean!*—for mean he must think me, if he imagines for one moment that I am capable of showing to Karl my disapprobation of his remarks, or of expressing regret to the boy at his uncle's action, or of lowering him in his nephew's eyes, and similar things!

"Nanni affirms that he must believe the contents of my letter. I doubt it, because it seems to me that if a person allows himself to grow so suspicious and distrustful of others, whom he knows from experience to be worthy of every confidence, then it is just as likely he will doubt, for a while at least, anything one might say to prove he is in the wrong. Perhaps he would judge differently, if he were aware of what I have done, or think about the matter; but that cannot be—I forgive him freely. It has pained and wounded me very deeply, and were it not for Pacher's friendship—I must say what I believe—I should be still more wretched than I am."

Beethoven's unfortunate habit of carrying out

his first impulse, and following up his first impressions in every-day affairs, often brought him into awkward scrapes. The young lady *à propos* to this habit of his, remarks:—"He vexed me once not a little by ascribing to me a misunderstanding he had with mother, which arose from my sister not being able to decipher something he wrote in a letter,—which, after all, was a very excusable mistake. But, I was somewhat surprised that he did not make any apology to me, after I had taken the trouble to explain in a long letter how the mistake had arisen, and how innocent I was in the matter. All he did was to raise his finger threateningly to my sister, and say, 'You will catch it for making such a mess of it!'"

The diary continues:—

"*August* 29*th.*—I can comfort myself with the assurance that Beethoven thoroughly recognizes the value of what we do for him, and a portion of our family at least have grown dearer to him since that unhappy affair. He is excessively genial and warm in manner to father and Nanni. I did not see him the time he was talking to Nanni at the gate. I feel as if, so to speak, he put me in the background. I dare say it only arises from my timidity. I try to forget what he has done lately, but I cannot, of course, help being still hurt that he so misjudged me. Nanni is of opinion that he will travel soon. I think his health is slightly better, but still his physical weakness greatly affects his powers of creation, and this determines him to yield."

The invitation to London had arrived, and Beethoven had replied early in July, that he would at once commence the composition of two great Symphonies. One was the exquisite, noble, and joyous Ninth, the other the unfinished Tenth of which so much was expected.

A considerable time elapsed before Fräulein Fanny again mentioned Beethoven in her diary, and then she merely inserts a slight notice of him.

"*November 10th.*—The day before yesterday we had a visit in the evening from Beethoven, who was pleasant and genial as of old. Our conjectures about that interesting friend of his are stronger than ever."

Who was the interesting friend here referred to? It was the beautiful and amiable Frau Marie Pachler-Koschak, of Graz, who, in the late summer of 1817, while visiting Vienna, was a great deal in Beethoven's society. She was young, highly educated, and very musical, and a note is still in existence in which Beethoven mentions her as "a true foster-mother to the creations of his brain," and rejoices that she intends staying a few days longer because then they "can have a great deal more music." But Anton Schindler, a young lawyer, who was continually with Beethoven about this time, and, later on, became so intimate with him, and so much in his confidence, that he undertook to write a biography of the great musician, intimates that there was a warmer feeling than mere friendship in the heart of Beethoven for this charming young lady, and speaks of it as an "autumnal love." The love of gossip, which especially extends itself over the actions of all famous men, no doubt stepped in here and carried reports to the Giannatasio family, which were conned over with an interest that was excessively natural, considering the affection and admiration some members of this household had for the great master. But the son of this "interesting friend," Dr. Faust Pachler, of Vienna, asserts that in Beethoven's admiration and friendship for his mother, there was no other feeling than the purest and strongest "artistic sympathy."

The diary continues:—

"*December* 23*rd*.—The day before yesterday I heard Beethoven's divine overture to 'Egmont.' Lotte was with me. I was carried away, as usual, with the charm of his creations, but I was impressed with the sad feeling that the man himself was *not* happy."

If she refers to any special sorrow which had lately fallen on the great master's shoulders, or is merely uttering her conviction on his life, as a whole, the young lady does not say. But a little song, composed at the close of the year 1817, gives us a tolerable insight into the feelings of the suffering deaf musician. The music is expressive of the state of his mind, and, heading it, was written on the MS., "To be played with feeling, but firmly, and well marked, the words to be distinctly recited;" showing that he deeply appreciated the incentive to his composition, and thanked the poet for his verses.

That from out of the shadow of such intense despondency, both as regards life and happiness, a high and lasting star of happiness should arise for Beethoven, was, of course, beyond the power of Fräulein Fanny to predict or recognise. But we are now in possession of the work which originated in this tomb of dark despairing sorrow. The Great Sonata, op. 106, was "inspired," as Beethoven termed the composition of his works at this time, and soon followed by the Grand Mass which was a foretaste of that sublime funeral hymn and rejoicing song of joy, the Last Symphony!

That the great musician was continually bringing himself into fresh entanglements, and thereby causing vexations and sorrow to those interested in him, we gather from the diary, the next entry in which we quote, under date of January 8th, 1818:—

"*Thursday.*—I was very much annoyed on Sunday by a proceeding of Beethoven's. He has not accepted father's proposal of keeping Karl with us on very reduced terms, neither has he informed us of his reasons for refusing. Hence, at the end of this month, we shall have to part from the boy, and, with his departure, one of the links which bind us to our beloved friend, Beethoven, who has lately caused us a good deal of trouble, will be snapped. I did not recognise at first why this gives me such intense pain. I know now that it was the manner in which it was done; the cold and formal, but extremely polite letter, without one particle of affection or interest for us expressed in it, has pained me more than I care to own. He tells father that Karl will be fetched when the time arrives for his departure; as, most likely, he himself will be away travelling, and the whole tenor of the letter shows so plainly his utter absence of regard for our feelings, and for any claim we may have on his consideration, that this parting with Karl is made a veritable grievance to us."

The letter referred to above is dated January 6th, 1818, and is as follows:—

"P. P.—In order that there may be no misunderstanding in the matter, I take the liberty of informing you that, unfortunately I must keep to the arrangement already made, and withdraw my nephew at the end of the month from your excellent Institution. As regards your proposal concerning my nephew, I have other intentions respecting his future, which, I trust, will be for his welfare; still, I must beg you to accept my thanks for your offer.

"It is just possible that Karl will be fetched somewhat earlier than at the stipulated time, and as I may be travelling myself, I will appoint some one to see to this for me. I tell you this now, that you may not think it strange on my part to send for him, when the time arrives for his departure. For the rest, both my nephew and I will ever through life be grateful to you.

I have already noticed that Karl feels gratefully towards you, which I take as a proof that, although he is thoughtless, he is not bad-hearted, and possesses no malignancy of disposition.

"I hope great things for him, all the more so since he has been for two years under such excellent guidance as yours."

The tone of this letter is certainly not that of great personal friendliness of feeling. Beethoven was evidently reserved in his expressions, because he felt that not only the Institution itself was defective, but that the education of the nephew—of whom he expected such great things in the future, and that his family "name was to be doubly honoured in him"—had not been all he could desire. Certainly, perhaps the intellectual training might have been defective in some respects, but the moral training and influence of this family over those under their charge, could not have been better or more conducive to the future welfare of the lad than it was, as we may judge for ourselves by every expression from the daughter's pen in the extracts we have taken from her diary. Beethoven must very soon have found out the mistake he made, and bitterly repented it in the after consequences. The withdrawal of his nephew from this influence was the immediate beginning of a sad and sorrowful career.

The diary continues:—

"*January 9th.*—Many domestic duties, and father's indisposition, which obliged me to remain by his side all the evening, prevented me, to a certain extent, from being able to give way to the low spirits I should otherwise have indulged in; for thoughts of Beethoven, to say nothing of my dark future, have made me feel very unhappy to-day."

"*January 24th.*—This morning Karl left us to take up his abode with his uncle. May he repay our beloved Beethoven all his devotion and self-sacrifice, by earnest application to his studies! The pain of parting was very much soothed by a warm and affectionate letter from his uncle."

Beethoven had written on the morning of the departure:—

"I will not come myself, because if I do it will appear more like a farewell, and all such scenes I avoid. Accept my heartiest and warmest thanks for the honourable and straightforward manner in which you have educated my nephew."

He intended calling on the family as soon as he was able, but, in consequence of various household arrangements, he did not resume his intimacy at the house, until driven to do so from necessity. The first notice of Beethoven in the diary does not occur till some months later on, and then it is written from Mödling.

"*June 15th.*—We hear nothing of Beethoven. When we were at Priel yesterday the time was too short for us to visit him. The country round looked charming."

The difficulties connected with his household, the new tutor, and so on, besides his own helplessness, we gather from various letters written during this summer of 1818. The verse beginning, "O hope! hope!" from Tiedge's *Urania,* he set to music in the spring of this year as a "theme" for his noble pupil, Archduke Rudolph. In a letter dated the 18th of June, addressed to Frau Streicher, the wife of Schiller's friend, whom he had known as a child in Augsburg, and who often solaced an hour for him in Vienna, he speaks of the difficulties he meets with in managing his servants, and of the renewed struggle he is daily called upon to go through with Karl's mother. "Everything is in confusion," he writes, "it will soon be necessary to send me to the madhouse. I have already gone through a great deal on this head, and things are not mending one bit." What had happened? Karl's mother had succeeded in corrupting the servants in Beethoven's house, and thereby obtaining secret intercourse with her son.

The young lady relates in her diary:—

"*September 9th.*—We spent Sunday with the Rohmanns, in the charming neighbourhood of Priel and Mödling. And we had a pleasant day, only it seems to me a great pity that I cannot rid myself of this painful feeling of loneliness which creeps over me, whenever I am not occupied with some duty. It is as if I felt the pain of a wound long since healed. In the afternoon we visited our ever-beloved Beethoven. He seems wrapped up in the care of his nephew, and more contented than formerly, especially when the mother is giving him no cause for sorrow. He expressed great pleasure at seeing us again, and said that as soon as he returned to town he would come and pay us a visit. He played to us on the English piano; not much, it is true, but still *Beethoven* played to us! Karl was not at home. I left, feeling more at rest about him, for I had had many doubts as to the state of his health, and I half feared his humour might have been unpleasant towards us."

The pianoforte referred to here was one of Broadwood's, which had been given to him by several brother musicians in London. He naturally played something on it to show off its perfections to his visitors, hence the reason for his playing at all.

The next extract gives us an insight into the cause of a further perplexity.

"*November 7th.*—Beethoven came to see father to-day. He has just returned from the country, and is sending Karl to the public school."

Which means to say that the lad, at twelve years of age, had entered the University! Fresh conflicts arose out of this step between the mother and the guardian, for the young boy took advantage of the confidence placed in him, and made use of his freedom and independence to an extent that was never intended by his uncle. The young lady anticipates fresh trouble for she writes:—

"*November 17th.*—Beethoven was with us again yesterday. We obtained a housekeeper for him. He was with us for three hours, during which we carried on our conversation in writing, for his deafness was worse than usual. One cannot be long in his company without being struck with the peculiar nobility of his character, and the high moral standard which animates all his actions, and pervades his every sentiment. How I hope that Karl will repay him in the future for all his present self-sacrifice! though I cannot help feeling a sort of *presentiment* that he will not! Beethoven talks of going to London in the spring: perhaps it will be a great advantage to him, from an economical point of view."

Beethoven instinctively visited the Giannatasio family rather often about this period, for in the order and peace of the household, he not only found rest and enjoyment for his weary spirit, but the sympathy and friendly attention he so surely needed.

"*November 20th.*—Yesterday we had a pleasant day with Beethoven. Nanni and I plucked up courage and practised our singing in his presence, when, behold! he, whom we thought had neither ears nor eyes for anything at the moment, but the engravings of Hogarth he was poring over, drew near while we were singing our first duet, and, what is more, remained by us. He grew interested in our performance, and now and again played or sang with us, which certainly sounded rather comical, as he was not always able to seize the exact tone. Still it helped us in giving the right expression. We both regretted very much that we had never summoned up courage to do this before, and thus had lost many an hour's enjoyment which we might have had, during the evenings he has spent with us. No doubt now he will soon be going to England, for he has received a second invitation to London. He was very pleasant indeed with us, and I was quite happy. Nanni showed him the things she has bought for her future home. How I hope he will come and see us often! He cannot fail to notice how pleased we always are to have him."

Then the young lady writes from memory:—

"Beethoven often indulged in small sarcasms, and once when our father remarked to him, 'My daughters can play your music,' he laughed. That was quite enough for us, and from that time forward, music was a tabooed sound in our drawing-room during his visits. I have regretted this over and over again, since one day, when I thought he was reading the journals in an adjoining room, I got over my shyness and began playing his 'Kennst du das Land.' I had not proceeded through many bars when he came into the room, stood by me, marked the time, and made me play one passage in crescendo which is generally performed somewhat slower."

"*November* 30*th*.—The day before yesterday, I was not only quite upset, but deeply pained by the account Beethoven's housekeeper gave us of his nephew's bad conduct. It is worse than thoughtlessness. Bad inclinations are evidently not to be eradicated by the force of good example! I cannot express the sorrow this ingratitude of Karl's causes me. But it is necessary to inform Beethoven of the sad truth, in all its stern reality, however much it may pain us to do it, and at whatever risk we may run of displeasing him in his present unhappy state of mind. If it only could be done quickly, it is of so much importance. He knows the boy is thoughtless, but he is not aware of these sad traits of a *corrupted* heart; but he must be told them, otherwise, it will be too late, if it is not so already. A letter will be the best way of doing it. Ah! if only I were a man, that I might become his most intimate friend!"

The further communications on this subject by this deeply sensitive lady are of true psychological importance. The following extract from the diary was evidently, judging from the writing, written under great personal agitation :—

"*December 5th.*—The last day or two, I am quite upset with this affair of Beethoven's. Never shall I be able to forget the moment when he came and told us that Karl *had left* him, and had gone to his mother, and he showed us the letter as a proof of his nephew's bad conduct. To see this man weeping, who has already had so much sorrow to bear, was one of the saddest scenes I ever witnessed.

"I remember Beethoven's exclaiming, with the tears running down his cheeks, in reply to our expressed sympathy, when trying to comfort him : ' Ah, but he makes me ashamed !' "

Then she goes on to add :—

"Father went actively to work, taking a great deal of trouble on his own shoulders, and, amidst all the trouble and sorrow of this affair, it is a pleasure to me to know that Beethoven leans upon us; indeed, for the moment, we appear to be his sole and only refuge. He must see now that he wronged us, if ever he judged us harshly in his mind. Ah! I am afraid that he will never comprehend how much we would do to help him; how intensely I long to make him happy. What a very strange and peculiar man he is! By means of the police, he has found his nephew, whom he has with him now. What an unnatural mother that woman is! It is fearful to me to think of all the sorrow these sad doings entail on our beloved friend! The upshot of this affair is that either he or she must leave the town. Beethoven wishes first of all to place the poor misguided boy under our custody for a time at least; which plan, if carried out, will be a great act of friendship on father's part, as he will have to keep watch over Karl as if he were a prisoner!

"Nanni and I have just been talking with Beethoven for several hours, or rather we have had to write everything we wished to say, for, when he is upset, as he has been lately, he hears nothing at all. We must have written a book-full at least. What a generous, pure, childlike soul he is! That such a man should be unhappy in life, is a great grief to me! He cannot comprehend that it is possible for a person to be so thoroughly wicked at heart, and by nature, as this woman is. I was glad when he said on leaving us that we had done him good. He told me that this affair had taken such hold of him that he had been able to hear his own heart beating all night long, and that he must try and collect his thoughts before he should be fit to do anything.

"It does seem rather hard that I, who would give half my life to save him from misery, dare not say a word more to comfort him than that we will all do that we can to help him, little as that help may be.

"He groaned over the state his housekeeping would be in on Karl's departure.

"One very terse remark of his, applying to the nourishment of the physical system, struck me as very sensible. He holds that to indulge in more than is necessary at the table, is a robbery of that part of our nature which requires the most attention, especially against the supplies needed for the mind!"

Again, in the following extract, we have a proof of the unbounded love and weakness of this man for his unworthy nephew, which, unfortunately, brought about fresh perplexities:—

"*Monday, 14th.*—Yesterday evening, I was called upon to realise the painful fact that it is quite impossible for us to win Beethoven's entire confidence; and, after the genuine proof we have given him of our devoted friendship, to act towards us as he has done, is distrustful and suspicious beyond endurance. We have had Karl with us for nine days, and, according to his uncle's wish and agreement made with father, he has been kept a close prisoner, and not allowed to mix with the other pupils on account of father's responsibility, and for fear of his corrupting them. And now Beethoven writes to say that we ought to have Karl's room kept warmer, as the boy has never been accustomed to have cold hands and feet; that he never meant him (Karl) to be so severely treated; and that he thinks the delinquent has been punished quite enough, and that by continuing such severity matters will perhaps turn out worse in the end!

"Hence, in his weakness towards the boy, he believes in him, whom he knows to be a liar, rather than trust his tried friends. I felt very bitter about it yesterday, but to-day I only feel pity for a man who has brought misery on himself by his own actions; and who must, if he reflects at all, realise that this is the chief reason why he is so *alone* in the world. Father wrote to him this morning, giving him fully to understand his own opinion in the matter: *perhaps* he will *understand* us in the future.

"This afternoon Beethoven met Nanni as he

was returning from the school, and took the boy from her. What will be the end of it all? One cannot but prophecy evil to come! Beethoven's weakness with regard to Karl is very great; the lad, no doubt, is very necessary to him, but it is a pity! I remember that once when I begged him not to put any faith in Karl's words, and not to yield in his decision of taking him from here, after ten times repeating that it would be of no use, he replied, "You think I am weak? Don't believe that," &c.

Very soon matters became worse. On the 10th of January, 1819, the young lady writes:—

"Müller has made us very unhappy by telling us of Beethoven's troubles. That wicked woman has carried matters so far as to triumph over him. He has *been relieved* of his *guardianship*, and his disgraceful nephew has gone back to his mother. I can imagine Beethoven's sorrow. Since yesterday evening he has been all alone; has had neither one nor the other with him at table. He ought to know that Karl rejoices in being with his mother; perhaps it will soften the agony of the parting to him."

The mother had sought to dispute the nobility of the uncle and guardian's birth, as the whole affairs, connected with the minority of her son, had come before a tribunal of nobles, who were well aware of Beethoven's position and character, and placed them in the hands of a burgher tribunal who personally sided with her.

So the boy went back to her, and Beethoven had to choose another guardian. The first act of the new guardian was to express a wish for the boy to be placed at school, and, naturally, Beethoven immediately thought of his old friend Giannatasio. He stated the case to him, and, in order to discuss the matter fully, the family agreed to pay him a visit on a certain day at Mödling, where he was then staying. In the diary it stands:—

"*June* 18*th*, 1819.—The object of our journey to Mödling was to talk over Beethoven's earnest desire of placing his unruly nephew under our care again, but we refused. He told father that, in spite of the letter, he would come and talk it over. But he altered his mind when he had read the letter, and the boy was sent to Blöckling's Institute. Much as it pained us to refuse a request of Beethoven's, I am quite sure that we did the right thing, for we could have done no real good, and, perhaps, on the contrary, a great deal of harm."

Then a year passed away, in which there were many struggles and contentions on all sides, till, finally, Beethoven succeeded in regaining full control over his nephew. The result, however, of this will be best explained in a note written by Beethoven to his friend and pupil, Archduke Rudolph, to excuse his continual absence at the hour of his lessons.

"The continual troubles connected with my nephew, who is almost entirely devoid of any right moral feeling, is the chief cause of my absence," he writes. And then, further on, he adds, " and this state of continual trouble seems everlasting. I have no help, and see no way out of it! As fast as I build, the wind blows my hopes away!"

Quiet hours with the Giannatasio family were a luxury very rarely indulged in. "Troubles, and various circumstances connected with our own family, seemed to separate us so much from Beethoven that, at last, we rarely heard of him," the young lady observes once herself.

But there came a time when Beethoven proved that he had not forgotten the existence of the heavy debt-book, wherein all the care and kindness bestowed on his nephew had been religiously written down. He had promised Nanni, of whom he often said, "She does not want me, she has her lover!" that he would compose her a song for her wedding, and, as the time drew nigh, he set to music for her a song with a chorus, the words of which were written by one of her father's friends, a Professor Stein. It began: "Auf Freunde, singt dem Gott der Ehe!"

The manuscript is dated the 14th of January, 1819: in the midst of his very worst troubles.

If one takes into consideration that, beside the grief and sorrow his nephew's want of moral principle entailed upon him, he was absorbed in the composition of his Grand Mass at this special time, and that naturally he had neither thoughts nor inclination for other things, the composition of this little festival song ought to be regarded as a decided and genuine proof of the great master's gratitude towards this family, to whom he owed so much. We are not informed of his presence at the wedding, hence we may conclude that, as he himself once said, his "face had no right among happy faces;" he was not there, for he was anything but "happy" at this special season.

Henceforth the diary contains only a few notices of Beethoven, but one of which is of any very great interest. But, before inserting it, we will venture to quote two passages which clearly express the deep and penetrating influence music, and especially Beethoven's compositions, had on the mind of this young lady who says it was the expression of her *being*, the *life of her soul.* This was the foundation of the intense personal yearning she had in her heart for his happiness; for, on the other hand, the old tempest-torn, misanthropical, suspicious man, who had shut himself out from all social joys, had very few of the ordinary attractions of mind to offer. It was the deep, inborn spirit of the German nation, and especially that of the Austrians, which was stirred to its very depths by Beethoven's music, and answering, so to speak, to every note of his compositions, by a thrill of sympathetic feeling.

The first passage reads as follows, and is dated Thursday, November 18th, 1819:—

"Gloomy ideas like dark clouds keep rising in my mind, now that we have music in our house again after four years' silence. What a change! Ehlinger dead; Götz, the soul of our society, away; Rohmann, Clarisse, and Nanni married; Duncker absent, and my mother broken down in health! I feel like a ghost wandering in empty halls. But above and around me hovers that Divine spirit which lightens the darkness of my path by its heavenly radiance. Ah! music, music! but for thy soothing influence how very intense would be my loneliness!"

And the second passage, dated the 17th of April, 1820, runs:—

"Yesterday I again heard the compositions of the two greatest masters of harmony, a new overture of Beethoven's, and the overture to 'Figaro' of Mozart. How the exquisite harmony of these divine compositions filled my soul with rapture, and penetrated me with the highest longing to worship the men, the inspired beings who created such marvellous works! We have arranged to pay Beethoven a visit very soon. I regret, infinitely more than I can express, that circumstances have so ordered it that our paths are separated—he always gave me so much heart and soul enjoyment."

The visit took place a couple of days later, after the mention of which, there is no further notice of Beethoven in the diary.

"*Wednesday, 19th April.*—This evening we paid Beethoven a visit. It was the first time we had seen him for a year. I fancied he was very glad to see us. He seemed tolerably well, and, at all events, he has a respite from the worries and torment of Karl's mother. It pained me terribly to realise that all our relations with this highly-gifted being are to a certain extent ended. His deafness has increased so considerably, that every word communicated to him had to be written down. He made me a present of a new song of his, which gave me immense pleasure."

This song, entitled, 'Abendlied unter dem gestirnten Himmel,' is dated the 4th of March, 1820, and is a very good sample of the strange, melancholy state of mind he was in at the time of its composition, when overcome with grief and sorrow he seemed filled with a presentiment that a deeper sorrow than he had yet been called upon to bear, was in store for him in the future.

The diary itself is continued up to the end of the year 1824, but there is nothing concerning Beethoven following the last extract we have mentioned above.

"When he met my mother, after the departure of his nephew, and the link between him and us had been thus snapped asunder, he took her hand, and, while pressing it, heartily remarked, ' Yes, I know, I ought to visit you,'" the young lady relates somewhere else. But he did not go to the house, and on both sides the complication of various outside circumstances prevented their old relations being renewed, till, in Beethoven's case, at least, death, in his fifty-seventh year, loosened the knot of life which he had in vain struggled to undo himself.

Neither is there any reference in the diary to the great concerts which took place on the 7th of May, 1824, wherein the last great works of the master, the Grand Mass and *Ninth Symphony* were produced before the public, and received with overpowering delight.

As time passed on, the young lady had the sorrow of hearing that his painful forebodings were realised respecting the result of the great love Beethoven bestowed on his nephew. A few years following that last notice of hers, misfortune upon misfortune had so accumulated upon the head of the young man by his own wilful acts, that, at last, there appeared to him no way out of the dilemma he was in, but to attempt to take his own life.

The news of this attempted suicide flew swiftly over the town, and excited and stirred all those both far and near who had formerly taken an interest in the law processes between the mother and uncle, and were aware of the sorrow the nephew had brought upon his gifted uncle—and, according to the view they took of these troubles, so they gave sympathy and fellow feeling to Beethoven, or heaped upon him reproach and bitter accusation. But Beethoven himself had to drink the cup to the dregs, which his own weak affection had helped to fill. And the extracts we have taken from the diary amply testify to the manner in which this affection was shown. He never recovered the shock of his nephew's act, and an eye-witness who saw him when he was barely fifty-six years of age, wrote of him: " Formerly he was healthy and robust; now an old man stood before us whose appearance denoted seventy years of age, shaking and bending beneath each gust of wind."

Fräulein Fanny's last painful impression of the friend she had so intensely admired is related by her from memory, in which she bemoaned not being able to visit the great master during the illness preceding his death, which lasted over a period of many months. "He had a great objection to female visitors all the time, and would see no one," are her own words.

And the great master himself: what happened during his last days? What was his end?

The perusal of this diary has brought us into such intimate relations with the circumstances which formed the most human element in his life, and most deeply influenced his own existence, that, in drawing the whole to a close, we must endeavour to clearly understand the distressing series of events which formed the catastrophe of Beethoven's life, and, putting aside reserve, examine the case closely. Thus, in spite of all that is repellent to our inner feelings, we may hope to close this sketch of one phase of his existence by leaving a consolatory impression behind, and recover our own footing by a free survey of the wide field of human existence. For the closing period of a man's life is the touchstone of the whole.

CHAPTER VI.

THE TRAGICAL END.

" Eine Stille suchte der Liebe Schmerz,
 Wo es recht wüst und einsam wäre;
 Da fand er denn mein ödes Herz
 Und nistete sich in das leere."
Goethe.

BEETHOVEN wrote on the 1st of June, 1801, to Amenda in Courland:—

" He and —— cannot get on together; he is, and always will be, too weak for friendship. I look upon him and —— as mere instruments, upon which I play when I please, but they can never be really witnesses of my inward and outward activity, nor are they capable of sympathy with me. I value them only for the services they render me."

This confession, written to his intimate friend,

indicates the point of view, from which, in the consciousness of his own unbounded power, and the Titanic efforts of which he was capable, he not only regarded, but very often treated those who surrounded him. He felt himself on the other hand "too strong for friendship," and thus it followed that, as in his artistic creations, so also in his deeper feelings and claims, he stood "alone in the world," and, as he thought, "had no friend."

The heroic defiance with which he encountered life, and even controlled circumstances, added to a sense of independence, such as appears in the notices in this diary, and which was at variance with the laws of human society, could not fail in time to turn him aside from the common path where friendship and love move along with gentle and modest steps, while steadily securing the progress of the race. Then, when suddenly in his later years, the ordinary duty of acting and caring for another was again forced upon him, it became evident that in his lofty aims this lowly gift found no place, or that he was incapable of exercising it. He entered upon it with his noblest efforts. But, as he substituted his own self-will for the fundamental laws laid down by life itself, the natural consequence was that evil was sown instead of good, and that, in spite of all weeding and uprooting, it flourished so as to threaten to choke the noble plant of the better nature.

We should know Beethoven but imperfectly if we did not pursue the track of his inner life hitherto almost undetected, and only revealing itself in his art. "It is all one, whether we are high born, or low born; human nature must have its vent," says the philosopher, so skilled in the study of humanity, who has given us the vivid personification of some of its phases in 'Faust.' Therefore it is that we seek to penetrate into this portion of Beethoven's nature, and to inquire whether it was the humanity in him which had to find vent in these bitter sufferings. As he did not really value the steady friendship of the Giannatasio family, and only answered them according to the services they rendered him—as the self-sacrificing devotion of the "lady abbess" was not recognised by him, and the violet blooming at his feet was utterly disregarded, so his obstinacy in his relations to the nephew and his disreputable mother, led to a whole series of arbitrary acts, which soon annihilated all possibility of mutual understanding.

It is needless to say that we have no intention of exonerating the nephew or his mother from the charge of the most culpable levity and complete unworthiness. But one thing is evident. Beethoven, with his exalted ideas and claims, weighed like an Alp upon the character of his young nephew, and never gave him a chance of natural self-development. Confusion, despair, rebellion followed, and it was the one last struggle of his better nature which led to that fearful attempt to commit suicide.

It is a curious psychological mystery which lies before us here, and every attempt to unravel it seems like an accusation and a reproach. Yet, for the sake of the recognition of a higher law, which leads us again from darkness into light, the inquiry must be made, or rather attempted.

The truth is that Beethoven's mind was exclusively bent upon high deeds of intellect and power, and, in his Titanic wrestling for the highest things, he disregarded that modest, simple goodness which, after all, constitutes the mainstay of life. Pure sacrifice of personality to the nearest and humblest aim of human existence, not only forms the happiness and elevates the nature of the majority of our race, but also specially gives it worth and coherence.

In the storm of action, the law of life had never presented itself to his mind, till it set before him in this instance the problem of duty, and he broke down in the attempt to solve it. It is the tragedy of power and heroic spirit which is represented in this artist-life, and finds its conflict and its catastrophe in the relations with his nephew. And the hero is seen in the artist, inasmuch as that, after recognising the all-conquering mystery, he plunges the spear into his own breast, and thus pays his free-tribute to the truth of humanity.

We add here as a guiding mark, the outpouring of heart which immediately follows in the diary, the cry of November 1819.

It is the confession no longer of a soul thirsting after sentiment, but it expresses the craving of the woman's heart.

The young lady writes:—

"Of my heart I will say nothing more; it is, and remains, empty: and this void is harder to bear than one would think. Sometimes the most cogent reasoning fails and feeling overflows. I cannot overcome it by force of thinking. The best course is to make up my mind that I can do nothing, alter nothing, and that, some day, perhaps, things will be better! I feel that no heart has ever beaten which longs so intensely and eagerly and so vainly for love, as mine does!"

As the plant yearns for light, as the hero pines for action, as the spirit bound down by hard necessity longs for freedom, so did this woman's heart yearn for love and active self-sacrifice. Although this was denied her, yet, as in her attachment to Beethoven, so in daily life, when years flowed onwards, she was moved by the impulse of her passionate nature to give freely to others that which she herself sought in vain. No truer testimony can be given of her after-life than the simple words of her niece:—

"She was so truly good and amiable, that *no* one could help loving her."

And another relative said of her, in reference to the cause for this sweetness of character, "Deep, true piety was the secret of her happy, contented life."

And the great master himself, what shall we say of him? For the interest of the world is fixed upon him who has given us so many hours of intense enjoyment, and not upon the obscure woman whose diary we have quoted. Did he learn to appreciate what lay at the root of her affection, and win it as a sweet possession for himself? and if not, why not?

But for this, why need we care to know that

a womanly heart was secretly devoted to him? The diary and its contents are only so far valuable to us as they give us the means of judging of this side of Beethoven's character, whether he was great as a man, as he is certainly the greatest of all composers.

The most superficial reading of this diary reveals to us its specific importance. For the reflection of a deep examination into Beethoven's nature, adds a fuller meaning to the preceding descriptions of the hero, in his noble struggle and his bitter suffering, his mighty creations, and his sensitiveness to all the happy gifts of nature. Although there is little of the ordinary artist-love to be found in this silent affection for Beethoven, yet we must not neglect to inquire into the deeper ground which made such devotion and true friendship possible, and finally led him to the most glorious goal.

Evidently he did not interpret correctly the loving care which surrounded his "dear ward," and which sought to relieve him of every sorrow and trouble that could possibly be taken from his shoulders. Through all his celebrity and greatness, it never lost sight of the man himself, and, still further, in all the richness and excellence of his nature, it never forgot that he was after all but human! The very reason of his existence was his art, and to it he gave all the power of his mind, for the honour of the Divine, the Eternal, the Everlasting! What people gave to him or did for him he accepted as his due—as a free tribute he worked for them —created for their benefit his marvellous compositions. Why, then, should he not receive whatever they had it in their power to give?

But, just at the time when, through the presence of this much-loved boy, a new element in life was revealed to him, he addressed the following comprehensive lines to the lad's tutor:—

"I entreat you to give special attention to his ethical training, as it supplies the lever to all real worth; and, however people may deride and scorn moral goodness, Goethe and other great writers set a very high value on it, for without it no man can be really distinguished, and there can be no solidity in him."

The sad experiences which followed, penetrated so deeply into his inner nature, that he came gradually to take an altogether different view of life. The bold, youthful spirit was bent upon "compassing the world;" and the unbroken manly strength—which had dictated the almost presumptuous exclamation: "Power is the morality of those men who distinguish themselves above others, and this power is mine!"— learned by bitter experience how little youth and mere "power" avail to win happiness for ourselves, or to give it to others.

Great things were accomplished: still greater things were planned out in his brain. Praise and renown were won, and his contemporaries were not niggardly in acknowledging his genius; and yet what had he won for his inner life? What had he gained to satisfy the craving of his heart?

"Love is a free-will gift!"

he exclaimed to himself when he underlined

those words of Goethe's, "West-östlicher Divan," which appeared in 1819.

"Have you been patient with every one to-day?" he wrote in his journal, in 1820; he who had once felt himself "too strong" for friendship—and then there awoke within him a hitherto unknown yearning for a true happiness, a desire to clasp to his heart the tangible possession of a living, breathing, sympathising being.

The more the outer gifts dropped away—and in the later years of the great musician's life they did drop away in a truly sad manner—health, material wealth, and every human comfort, even glory and fame, for, from the year 1820, the same Vienna which had boasted Gluck, Mozart, Hadyn, and shouted applause to Beethoven, made an idol of Rossini! The more, then, outer success flagged, and he learned by experience that life needed other treasures than power and fame, all the keener became his yearnings for the true treasures of life. In spite of all the glories that his art and the

Muses lavished upon him, he felt an irrepressible void within. He had "no friend;" he stood "alone in the world!"

The purely human need, to call at least one human being his, enters into his life with the irresistible force of a natural desire.

And, although, as the young lady discovered, even with him and after the manner of his manly spirit, this need breaks forth with passion, and carries on, so to speak, its sport with the beloved object. However, we shall soon find that his own existence suffers shipwreck in the exaggerations and caprices of this love of his, but he recognises the law and acts upon it. Tried in a truly human way, he preserves his own human individuality, and forces the sting of humanity deep into his own heart, to the very root of his own life: but he has grasped the eternal and comprehensive meaning of this law of mankind, and penetrated the fulness of its happiness.

And now, what more?

Even here he sings of his sorrows, of his joys. If we have over-estimated his pictures of life, of the public, and of his own private life, and found in them the immortal echo of all the movements of our existence—more, infinitely more, is what he now sang out of the depths of this root of our existence. No artist has ever penetrated deeper, for none has ever thrust the thorn of life deeper into his own heart, and won, by the surrender of it, his success and his immortality.

For if we look to the later expression of his genius, glorious as are the 'Sonata Pathétique,' the one in D flat, and the 'Apassionata,' in their expression of the full power of life; grandly as the 'Eroica' announces a new order of things, and the Symphony in C minor conveys the certainty that, in the struggle of human will with fate, human power must finally conquer; nobly as the Seventh proclaims this victory, and joyfully depicts the whole magic and glow of the fulness of life; what are all these glories of outward existence, these hopes and plaints compared to the cry of the soul, the echo of the deepest order of the things themselves, which rings in Beethoven's works after life, which appeared to have raised him to its heights at the Congress of Vienna, now first showed him its true lessons and its real suffering!

"O guide my soul; O lift it out of this depth of sorrow!" we hear him cry, and he chisels this cry of the soul, so to speak, into a monument in stone, for all posterity to behold, in the Adagio of the Violin Sonata, op. 102, Number II. In this work no sensitive human heart can fail to recognise its humanity, or to carry away out of deep resignation to the crushing force of existence, the revelation of a higher life. For: "He is above all things! Without Him is nothing!" was written shortly after in his diary. And what worship to "Him above" is the Adagio of that Great Sonata, op. 106, which appeared in the midst of those "distressing circumstances," caused by the struggle in his relations with mother and son in the time from 1817–18, which we seem personally to live through, in the records of an impartial third party!

But if such an Adagio is only an individual

prayer, though an inimitable one, we soon find the artist, who could extend his feelings to the whole of mankind, uttering a prayer of humanity, in which all voices of life unite, to mourn his sad lot and implore help from on high. A great soul concentrates itself, to become the representative of all the suffering that weighs down mankind. And truly, if ever an artist was trained by the experience of life to feel the dignity of such a vocation, to lend his voice to the universal prayer, it was Beethoven.

"Sacrifice once more all the trivialities of social life! A God over all!" we hear him cry, when the graceful duty was laid upon him of celebrating with his art a decisive event in the life of his loved Imperial friend, Archduke Rudolph, and he prepared to write a solemn Mass for his installation as Archbishop of Olmütz.

We know what this Missa Solennis is, which issued out of years of deepest contemplation and torturing struggle. It stands like a colossal Cathedral, in the style of a bygone age indeed, but freely and boldly employing the received forms, and often breaking through, as it were, like a beam from above, to show the great human personality of the artist, who feels himself safe near to "Him above," and presents to us the well-known features in a new and transfigured light.

But what is that which arches itself visibly to heaven, rising to all height and spreading far and wide, as though it could embrace all existence, and concentrate all the movement of life into one grand whole?

It is the majestic hymn, Et vitam venturi, 'An eternal life!' an image of that eternally flowing and inexhaustible fulness of the Divine power, carrying us away till our senses are in an ecstasy, as no art ever before did! What a vision of the Eternal must here have been given to the artist, to support him against the pressure of transitory things. We can now understand that this man had often no eye and no ear for the things of life, and in the storm of his inspirations carried this little life forcibly with him, into a higher sphere.

But this actual life has its own laws, and its claims will not be silenced by the greatness of intellectual rapture. And this bold wrestler, with all his manly spirit, had to acknowledge this with bitter heart-experience: to this phase of his spiritual development we owe his highest creation, the triumphant prize of human happiness wrought out of suffering.

We approach the Ninth Symphony, and its meaning will reveal to us the image of this artist and man, since it contains the secret and the outcome of his whole life.

Happily in this case we possess, and more certainly than at other times, the stand-point of the artist's own course of thought and feeling; the plan in detail of the work itself. We must make it clear to ourselves; it is, in a manner, the inner history of Beethoven.

We know that the work closes with the choruses on Schiller's 'Freude, schöner Götterfunken.' Long ago in Bonn, when the spirit of modern time, rather than of reviving humanity revealed itself in vivid forms to his lofty youthful aspirations, this outpouring of the soul of the glorious poet had so attracted him, that he determined to compose music to the whole poem. His heroic spirit foresaw that there would be an outcome somewhere, that somewhere the "flag of joy would move." He foresaw it, without clearly recognising that end, that goal, distinctly as the poet's instinct had expressed it. And this image again and again returns to his mind: and in the Seventh Symphony he thinks of writing an overture on the several verses of this poem.

But it was fated that the needs of our race should leave their mark upon him, before he could rise to this joy. We have seen his wrestlings, we have heard his prayers for mercy to "the most unhappy of all mortals." He fights a gigantic battle, he raises his soul to the vision of an eternal necessity, in which his own struggle and agony disappear. And he here throws into music these imaginations, these strivings of his deepest self. He succeeds in penetrating to the inner harmony, and recognising the rift in our whole human existence, but also he charms away the spell which lies upon it.

But, artistically and psychologically, no more difficult problem was ever set before him, than to find the right way here. We have the proof of this in his own note-books.

Above all, there is one which concerns the introduction of this "Joy." This Finale was begun in the most concentrated feelings of human suffering, and, as it were, fiendish scornful laughter at all human joy. "No, this labyrinth reminds one too much of our desperate position!" is to be read, so far as we can decipher the illegible pencilled manuscript. It is the remembrance of the fearful struggle which in the first movement his lofty courage held with fate, with inexorable necessity, which here reveals to us what he had suffered from the sorrow of the world.

"This is a solemn day, let it be celebrated by song and dance!" he says further on, and then introduces the motive of the first movement.

"Ah no, this is too melancholy. I want

something more cheerful." Then appears the motive of the Scherzo : " This is all nonsense ! " —of the Adagio : ' This is too soft, too tender." And, at last, when the stormy burst of the introduction returns, he says : " Friends, we have reason to despair; but I believe music must console us, cheer us."

Thus the artist has admitted us into his workshop, the man into the mystery of his feelings. For when Beethoven speaks of music as a consoler, we are reminded of the words of the greatest composer of our own times, who has followed most closely in his track: "I cannot grasp the spirit of music otherwise than in love."

And now, when we examine the work itself, what is all that Beethoven has hitherto sung, compared with the human lament, and the yearning after a human existence, in the first three movements of his Ninth Symphony ?

Through all the ecstasy of spiritual vision, and all the triumph of artistic creation, the natural longing to perfect our life in that of another, had never been absent from his heart. And the strains which flow from this longing, ring with an echo out of the very depths of human yearning, never before heard.

"What was that?" we ask ourselves unconsciously when the two melodies in the Adagio of this Symphony are heard and exercise their irresistible power over us. "Have I ever felt, suffered, asked myself, what ecstasy and happiness are, what intense longing for both?" echoes in our inmost soul.

The sorrow of the world is pursued into the most distant hiding-places, a brave fight is fought against the overspreading grey fog of negation; life itself is a mere farce, the wild passion of enjoyment only, the gratification of desire; and even the prospect of an eternal and infinite joy out of ourselves, with all its glory and Divine harmony, does not still the longing of the heart for possession of itself!

So then this artistic and human eye has penetrated into all the most remote and secret corners of human existence, and recognised what joy and happiness, what an infinite outflow of love is to be had in this world of cruel privations and insatiable selfishness, and can make of this barren world a heaven itself.

"For life is love!"

Beethoven had underlined in the "West-östlicher Divan," and more deeply than all who had preceded him, was he to grasp this meaning of human existence, and bequeath it to us in his art as a prophecy and a consolation.

"O Friends, not these tones, but let us raise some more joyful and hopeful!" he exclaims yet again in the full outburst of natural feeling in the Finale. And now peals forth, as if born out of some sorrowful renunciation, and yet with victorious confidence of certainty that there is an ever-fading happiness, that song of true humanity:

"Freude, schöner Götterfunken,
Tochter aus Elysium!"

It is the very human soul which has found itself here. The young lady's words: "Never has a heart beaten that has longed so eagerly and so vainly for love as this one," finds its truth here in the higher sense of existence for the sake of the race : it is love for all mankind which has become active as the highest capacity for work and happiness, and no child's joy is purer, rings more clearly, than this joy of men in such individual existence. Beethoven completely reveals himself to us in this melody, and we gather from it the highest joy of his life, as well as the sorrows which had preceded it.

He has at last found what he sought with such earnest prayers and tears : the Almighty, Eternal, Infinite Truth. "He is above, and without Him is nothing." How has that certainty of a Divine power in this world, found its full and blessed confirmation. This is no dream, no fancy, no deception. What Schiller expressed in the way of aspiration, and as echoing a wide-spread feeling and conviction, has here become reality—clear tones out of the heart of a true man and lover of men.

And how certain he is of this foundation of

true happiness and steadfastness in a sorrowful despairing world!

> "Seid umschlungen, Millionen,
> Diesen Kuss der ganzen Welt!"

Such an intense realisation of life in love sounds in solemn tones as the ground of that joyous "Divine Spark," and at the same time as its fulness and durability. Here is solved the mystery of happiness and unhappiness; here lie truth, fulness, and eternity; in short, real life.

Seldom has an artist evolved the reality of the world more purely and deeply through his own feelings, seldom expressed it so clearly and ennoblingly. He raises by the power of a mighty vision his own being out of the limitations of his personality, and gives himself and us a share in an immortal possession.

In complete forgetfulness of the world, this hymn of joy which flows from love, had been composed in the summer and autumn of 1823. And that it was irresistible in its grandeur and joyfulness, as if indeed its joy had taken possession of the world, was proved by the effect of its first production in 1824. The excitement of the thousands of listeners was like a storm passing over the sea. "The people broke out into such shouts that the orchestra was almost inaudible; tears stood in the eyes of the performers," relates one of the instrumentalists.

Only Beethoven heard not the tumult of applause. When his attention was called to it, he looked up and bowed quite calmly.

What was the recognition of even the most musical and sympathetic audience in the world, as the public of Vienna certainly must be called —what was this to him compared with that of "one soul," really capable of understanding him, of comprehending his highest aspirations, and, through them, his art?

The fragment of conversation between him and his nephew on this occasion, tells more than their long reports and descriptions.

Beethoven.—"How did you feel during my music—the same as others seem to feel?"

Nephew.—"Something deeper,—not merely striking the ear."

But the growing absorption in his own life and work, partly a necessity of his character, partly, alas! the result of actual pressing need to provide daily bread for himself and his "dear son," left the latter more and more to his own devices. And, as he had now been emancipated from the discipline of the Institute, and was attending the University, he soon became impatient of the control forced upon him by intercourse with his uncle and his great ideals; from idleness he passed to frivolity, and then to vice. As the young lady had feared, the ardent affection of Beethoven for the boy, and the wish to have "some one about him, who was really attached to him," not only led the uncle to relax the reins of authority, but to give way to the young man, so that he soon began to set at naught the wishes of his guardian. "O, my uncle! I can do as I like with him. A little flattery and a few friendly words will soon bring him round!" Such were his expressions, after Beethoven had ventured some well-meant remonstrances.

"Where am I not wounded, cut to the

heart?" we hear Beethoven cry. And, again, "O vex me no more. I have not too many years to live, as it is!" And this to the very boy to whom he confesses that if *he* is only loving, good and upright, his uncle's happiness will be complete. He has renounced all that life offers, but not all that constitutes life! And even this is denied to him,—him so full of love and so thirsting for love. It is the last and bitterest cup of sorrow.

Of this sorrow, the deepest that can stir the human breast, the master's own tones tell us, and, in spite of all that had hitherto been sung to that chord, most deeply, most originally, most touchingly. He who will rightly understand the whole nature of this artist, who will penetrate the fulness which flows out of these bitterest of sufferings, let him plunge with all the feeling of his soul into the marvellous spring of the last quartette, Beethoven's Swan song!

Here, more than anywhere else, the most secret movements of the human soul reveal themselves;

joy and woe appear to flow from the same fountain. And there is no weak complaining, no unmanly expression of grief. The last sound is not desertion and death,—it is, spite of all sorrow and sacrifice, riches and life, inexhaustible life, and consciousness of immortality! Personal interest is given up; but the gain of the other, which is grasped with one's whole nature, is the gain of the whole, and of its undying, interwoven completion. As his art, so all the personal expressions of the master during these last years show an almost unearthly harmony and gentleness, which poured itself out refreshingly on the little and daily narrowing circle of his friends, and left an indelible impression behind.

"You are the best of all,—all others are but trumpery," writes, in his simple view of the case, the young son of his friend Breuning, who often visited him in his last illness, and cheered him with his young, fresh feelings.

So he lived then, as good as separated from the outer world, but all the happier in his own world, which now first yielded to him clear visions and inspirations. And so men saw him walking dreamily along, and let him go, as we let a man go, who belongs to another existence.

An author, residing at Vienna, who was acquainted with Franz Schubert, saw Beethoven in these later years spend many a winter evening in a little inn. All were "full of the greatest respect" when he came in, the man "from whose lion head streamed grey locks like a mane," who, on entering, cast around a sharp look, but wavered in his movements, "as if he walked in a dream."

So he went in, sat down to his glass, smoked out of a long pipe, and closed his eyes. When spoken, or rather shouted to by an acquaintance, he opened his eyelids like an eagle startled out of sleep, smiled sadly, and handed the speaker a memorandum book with a pencil, which he drew from his breast-pocket. After the question was answered, he sank again into meditation. But sometimes he took a thicker book out of the pocket of his old grey overcoat, and wrote with half-shut eyes.

"What is he writing?" inquired our informant, one evening, from his neighbour, Franz Schubert.

"He is composing!" was the answer.

Perhaps, in such moments, such tones passed through his mind as those of the first movement of the B sharp Quartette, op. 130, or those of the 'Poco scherzando' in the same quartette, in which all life has become a sport to the eternal powers. Or, again, that Cavatina in E, to him "the crown of all quartette movements and his favourite piece," and of which our informant, about the first representation of the Ninth Symphony, K. Holz, says: "He composed it literally with tears of sorrow, and confessed to me that never before had his own music made such an impression upon him, and that even the repetition of this movement always cost him a tear."

And yet this "fulness of joy and woe" was to be outdone!

The Quartette in C minor followed. And, like a quiet talk with oneself and with the innermost spirit of the world, begins the leading Adagio; the Andante, with its enchanting ever-varied pictures of life, follows like a gush of gladness; the final Allegro is like a dance of life itself, with all its fears and its joys, its perplexities, and its outburst of ecstasy. Like life itself, this wondrous musician is inexhaustibly fertile in his pictures of life.

But once it is as if he described, and for the last time, himself, and, at the same time sang his death-song. To understand this, we require a brief reference to his biography.

His nephew, grown into Beethoven's very life, and day by day more indispensable to his heart, had been expelled from the University in consequence of neglect of his studies, and had entered the Polytechnic School. But here, again, the difficulties to which we have alluded arose in the first term. Severe conflicts with his uncle followed. Yet full forgiveness and reconciliation ensued; Beethoven almost implored love from him who trod love under foot. Let any one read the letters of the autumn of

1825. Arrogance, calumny, confusion gained the upper hand. Still the conscience of the young man knocked loudly in the presence of the venerable uncle, knocked ever more loudly, and soon with unendurable and irresistible clamour.

Then came the worst, the most frightful thing that could happen here, for even the person of his great uncle was no longer sacred to him. The situation became insufferable; the youth attempted his own life, and the details of this deed reveal to us the underlying cause of this tragical conflict; tragical, because it bound the will equally on both sides.

We give the affair from the conversation-books here used freely for the first time. The discourse takes place for the most part between the government officer and the violinist, Karl Holz. He had made himself valuable and almost indispensable to Beethoven, by a variety of good offices. And though he was as far as anybody from expecting the catastrophe, he showed himself ready, at least outwardly, to comfort and help the old, helpless master.

It was about Midsummer, 1826. Karl had been living for a year at the house of a Herr Schlemmer in the Alleegasse. His chief friend and companion was a young man called Niemetz.

Holz rushes one morning into Beethoven's room, and tells him, on the part of Schlemmer, that Karl has left his house to shoot himself! They both hurry off to the Alleegasse. It is the most horrible day of Beethoven's life. The following conversation is at once begun with the deaf man:—

Schlemmer.—" Here is the long and short of it. I heard that your nephew intended to shoot himself, at latest next Sunday. I could only gather that it was on account of debts. I made a search, whether any preparations had been going on, and found in his drawers a loaded pistol, additional powder and shot. I sent you notice, that you might act as his father in the transaction; the pistol is in my charge. Deal gently with him, or he will be driven to despair."

Holz.—" What is now to be done ? Something worse will happen. He was not to be detained ; he said he would come again to Schlemmer; he was just running over to you. He said: ' What is the use of hindering me ? If I do not succeed to-day, it will be done some other time.'"

Schlemmer.—" My wife has the second pistol, because I was not at home when it was found."

Beethoven.—" He will drown himself!"

Holz.—" If he had really determined to destroy himself, he would certainly have communicated his intention to no one, least of all to a chattering woman. Perhaps a theatre-princess. You had once sent him Hufeland with your remarks ; how he protested against it! He was seen with her early in the morning at the Kärnthner Thor.

They hasten now along the high road to Niemetz's house; he is not at home. Then back to the Alleegasse, to the police-office. Here begins, through the medium of our interpreter, the closer interrogatory.

Holz.—" Does he wear rings, frock-coat lined with silk-collar, no watch ? We must send at once to the coffee-houses. To the mother's, then! We had better go home now; thence you can send to Schlemmer, and, after dinner, we will go to the mother."

Hours of terrible anxiety roll by. They return to the mother's, and there, at last, they discover very hastily written, in the pocket-book:—

Karl.—" Now it is done. Torment me no more with reproaches and complaints. Only a surgeon who will hold his tongue. It is all over. Everything can be arranged afterwards."

Beethoven.—" When did it happen?"

The Mother.—" He has just come; the coachman has carried him down from a rock at Baden. He has a ball in the left side of his head."

Beethoven then goes away with Holz, and we hear the following particulars:—

Holz.—" He said: 'If he would only cease those reproaches of his!' He wanted to shoot himself in the Helenenthal, upon a rock at Rauhenstein. He went yesterday from me straight into the city, bought a pistol, and drove to Baden. Here you see his ingratitude plainly, why try to restrain him any longer? Once in the army, he will be under the strictest discipline. When you went, he said: 'If he would only never show his face again!' I came here, just as he was seizing you by the chest, out at the door, when he wanted to go away. He said he would tear off the bandage, if another word was spoken about you."

All this drove so many dagger-thrusts into Beethoven's heart. But, for the moment, he has only one anxiety. For Holz had written: " It is still a question whether he can recover. A wound in the head is dangerous." And there was real anxiety about the life of the young man, the only human being whom he loved, and who—even in his present hatred he proved this—loved him, because he understood him more deeply than all the outside world.

About a fortnight after, we find, written in Beethoven's own hand:—

" On the death of the dead Beethoven."

Whether this regarded his nephew, or himself, who shall decide? But it is all one, for it was, in either case, his own life which was fatally wounded, and we shall soon hear his death-song.

A few more notes from the pocket-book, which carry us to the core of the thing.

Beethoven.—" One night at a ball, he did not sleep at home. The mother had gone to Presburg, or some other place. His mad gambling must be stopped, otherwise no improvement *is* possible. He has constantly played billiards with coachmen," &c.

Schindler.—" The gentlemen of the Polytechnic School have made use of the opportunity to warn him, because they have frequently seen him playing in coffee-houses with coachmen, and quite common people, with whom he often came off second best."

Holz.—" Although I have had experience enough of the doings of young people, it is scarcely credible in what complications they involve themselves. The waitress remarked that Niemetz and Karl had carried on all kinds of pranks together. Then an extract from Karl's letter to his friend: "How is your charming girl, your goddess? Have you seen her, and will you see her again? I have to write in much haste for fear of being discovered by old N——. It is enough, enough!"

Yet Beethoven writes: "I will still try to reform him. For, if he is left to himself, yet worse things may follow. More than any father! Confusion of mind and wildness, even from childhood, tormented with headache."

He visits him in the hospital. "If you have a secret trouble, reveal it to me through your mother." Holz had communicated: "He said it was not hatred, quite another feeling, which irritates him against you." And it was long before the boy succeeded in expressing his feeling. "He gives no other reason, but the imprisonment at your house, the existence under your surveillance," writes Holz; and Breuning, "He stated at the police-office, that it was your constant worrying him which had driven him to the deed."

At last we come to the full solution of the mystery.

"I have become worse, because my uncle insisted upon making me better!" he answered to the inquiries of the magistrate, after his recovery.

He who understood this word best was Beethoven, the great Beethoven. To spectators at a distance, and even to immediate associates of the master, an apocalyptic utterance; to himself, clear as the sun, and forcing its way into his heart like the prick of a guilty conscience! He died of this discord, which became more and more declared shortly afterwards.

But the unfortunate nephew was partially reformed by this catastrophe, and his uncle's death cleared yet more the atmosphere of his inner nature, and laid a check on his will. He married, and became a good husband and father. He developed in his married life the qualities which his great uncle had not known how to appreciate, and left behind him a family living in harmony, with the exception of one son, who inherited "his mother's blood."

And did Beethoven, in the consciousness that a law of nature had avenged itself, gain a part in the peace and satisfaction which this closer knowledge of the world and life can give?

"I was pained beyond measure at the sight of Beethoven," wrote that interesting woman, Marie Pachler-Koschak, at the close of 1823, and this was confirmed by one of Beethoven's reverential friends, who was a true helper to him in his later needs, Stumpf, the harp manufacturer, from London. He says, after revisiting his German home, and Beethoven: "It struck me at once that he looked very unhappy. And his *famulus*, Schindler, describes him as looking, after that last catastrophe, like 'an old man seventy years old, powerless of will, and obeying every breath of air.'"

When first Fate knocked threateningly at his door, he wrote, "You shall see me not unhappy, but as happy as it is permitted to me to be here below."

And so it was! Not only did he meet his

own death with "indescribable calmness," as eye-witnesses report, but he had also recovered the cheerfulness which is the inheritance of souls secure in themselves. He had gazed into the very essence of life, and his gain was "deep, true piety," the religion of love. The power and lasting nature of this possession sufficed him.

To illustrate all this more minutely is the office of biography. But the best expression of it is, after all, in his music. And here it was that he sang himself into peace and joy.

The years 1824–26 did not produce much, but the last quartettes contain a world of poetry and truth. The last real outpouring of his soul is the wonderful mysterious air of the last quartette (op. 135, F sharp) the ' Lento assai e Cantante tranquillo,' which arose in that time of intense anxiety about his beloved son, and has given us a better insight into the state of his mind, than all researches in conversation and note-books.

It is at once his death-song, and his noblest song

of life. No other could so announce the sorrow of his soul, no other the pure joy arising out of deep suffering. It is unequalled in earnestness and depth of feeling, as in grace and richness of form and movement.

Could we succeed in clothing the meaning of those tones in words, according to their gradual development, we should have the sense not only of this one work, but of Beethoven's whole nature, in one clear picture before us. But to see this we must call up the echoes of the tones themselves to lend their magic light to the picture. We give at the end of this work the melody of this Adagio, and advisedly add to it the German words which educe its inner meaning.

Perhaps in living song the living impress of Beethoven's nature may appear, which word and picture alone can never fully represent—his joy born out of suffering, in the happiness and permanence of our race, his silent love for mankind.

248 *AN UNREQUITED LOVE.*

Beethoven's Grabgesang.

Sehr langsam und ruhig.

Mü - de bin ich, geh' zur Ruh',

Hab' ge - nug ge - lebt, ge - lit - ten. Wund im Her - zen,

THE TRAGICAL END. 249

wund in Schmerzen, die das Le - ben mir ge-bracht.

AN UNREQUITED LOVE.

Hoch und kühn der Jugendmuth,
Ernst und treu des Mannes Streben:
Wollt' die ganze Welt umfassen,
Liebend bringen ihr das Glück.

Doch wer mag dem Leben nah'n?
Stürmend warf's mich aus dem Gleise.
Und von alle meinem Lieben
Blieb mir nichts als mein Gesang.

Doch ob auch zum Tode wund,
Will der Liebe Lied ich singen.
Denn die Liebe ist das Leben,
Liebe einzig Menschenglück.

Lösung aller Erdennoth,
Allumschlingen, Allerbarmen!
Lieb' ist Wahrheit, Lichtes Fülle,
Sel'ges Leber, ew'ges Sein!

Lightning Source UK Ltd.
Milton Keynes UK
UKHW02f0612060618
323809UK00004B/238/P